DETAILING
DIESEL
LOCOMOTIVES

Jeff Wilson

KALMBACH
BOOKS

About the author

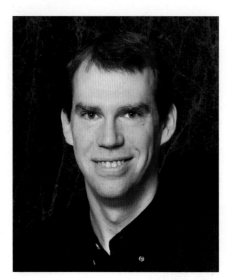

Detailing Diesel Locomotives is Jeff Wilson's 19th book on railroads and model railroading. Jeff spent 10 years as an associate editor at *Model Railroader* magazine, and he currently works as a freelance writer, editor, and photographer, contributing articles to MR and other magazines. He also writes a model railroading column for *Model Retailer* magazine and is a correspondent for *Trains* magazine. He enjoys many facets of the hobby, especially building structures and detailing locomotives, as well as photographing both real and model railroads.

Unless noted, photos were taken by the author.

Printed in the United States of America

11 10 09 08 07   1 2 3 4 5

Secure online ordering available: www.KalmbachBooks.com

Publisher's Cataloging-In-Publication Data
(Prepared by The Donohue Group, Inc.)

Wilson, Jeff, 1964-
   Detailing diesel locomotives / Jeff Wilson.

   p. : ill. ; cm.

   ISBN: 978-0-89024-700-6

1. Diesel locomotives--Models. I. Title. II. Title: Diesel locomotives

TJ630 .W542 2007
625.1/966

Contents

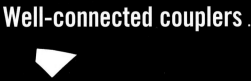

CHAPTER ONE

Realism: It's in the details

A handful of detail parts and decals turned a stock Proto 2000 E unit, left, into a more-accurate, more-realistic model, right.

Today's top-of-the-line, ready-to-run plastic locomotive models already feature sharp-looking paint schemes and an incredible level of detail. They may even have many separately applied details that until recently had to be added by modelers themselves. Do these improvements mean modelers can forget about customizing and detailing their diesels? Far from it. Even with high-end models, it's impossible for manufacturers to offer all detail variations for the thousands of road name and locomotive model combinations produced. Some factory-applied details aren't as accurate or realistic as those available from detail manufacturers.

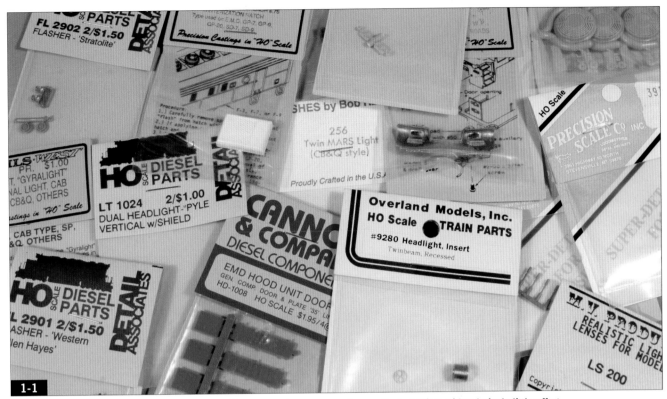

Detail parts from several model manufacturers allow you to improve your locomotive's realism with relatively little effort.

Match a prototype

In addition, many mid-priced models run well but don't have the extensive detail of their more-expensive cousins. With a handful of detail items and a few hours' work, modelers can transform these into unique models that more closely match specific prototypes.

Detailing models to match specific real locomotives is easier today than ever before, thanks to the thousands of after-market detail items available from manufacturers like A-Line, Cal-Scale, Cannon & Co., Custom Finishing, Detail Associates, Details West, Hi-Tech Details, Precision Scale, and others, **1-1**.

Many modelers think detailing can only be applied to undecorated models, which then require painting and decaling. However, as the models in chapters 2, 3, and 4 show, many detail upgrades – including some that require body modifications – can be accomplished on decorated models as well. In fact, most ready-to-run models can be enhanced by a few additional detail or decal items.

This book walks you through improvements in several models as inspiration for developing your own

modeling and detailing projects. The techniques shown apply to many other models, regardless of era or road name, not just to the models shown.

Finding information on the locomotive you want to model is the first step, **1-2**. If you're lucky, perhaps you can find a modeling article that lists part numbers and instructions. The magazine index on the trains.com Web site is a great place to start looking for modeling articles.

Also, look for photos of the real locomotive. Books, magazines, Web

Books, photos, magazine articles, and historical society publications are all handy references for detailing locomotives.

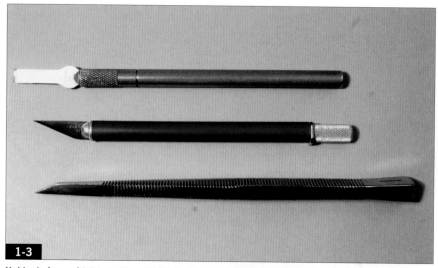

1-3

Hobby knives with blade Nos. 17 (top) and 11 are essential. The Micro-Mark modeler's chisel works great for removing molded details from body shells.

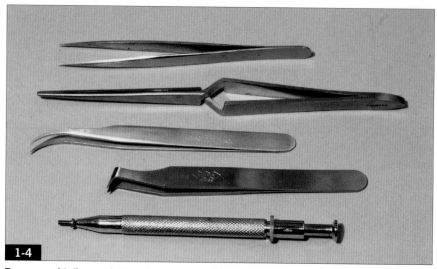

1-4

Tweezers with fine straight and curved tips hold small parts, and fine sprue cutters remove parts from sprues with little cleanup necessary. A screw holder is the best tool for holding and starting screws.

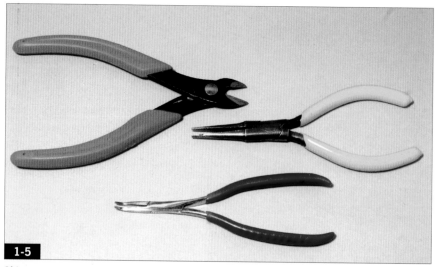

1-5

Side cutters work for cutting wire and trimming plastic, while needle-nose and fine pliers are good for holding small parts securely.

sites, and dealers offer black-and-white prints or color slides. Railroad historical societies may have back issues of their publications, many of which focus on specific locomotives or locomotive classes.

Examine the photos to determine the features of the locomotive and see how they compare to the details on your model. Compare the prototype features to available model parts. The Walthers catalog and Web site (www. walthers.com) are good places to start, as are the Web sites and catalogs of individual detail manufacturers (listed in the appendix).

Compile a list of the parts you need, make a trip to the hobby shop, and get to work!

Levels of detail

Many detail upgrades are simple, require a minimum of parts and work, yet still result in improved appearance. Other modifications require more time and work and can be more challenging. Your skills will improve as you tackle more and more projects, and many modelers find that their standards for acceptable levels of detail increase as they get better at it. You have to decide what's right for you.

If your focus is operation – especially if you run your models frequently – or if you transport models to club meetings or other layouts, you might settle on minimal detailing and sturdy detail parts that can handle the stress of moving. If it's locomotive modeling and detailing itself that interests you, you'll probably choose a higher level of detail.

Let's look at some of the tools and materials you'll need to get started.

Tools

You'll need some basic modeling tools – many of which you probably have already – along with a few more advanced or specialized tools.

For starters, you'll need hobby knives with No. 11 (long pointed) and No. 17 (chisel-tip) blades, **1-3**. Replace blades frequently, especially if the tip breaks or you notice more force is required to cut materials. If blades seem expensive, look for economical

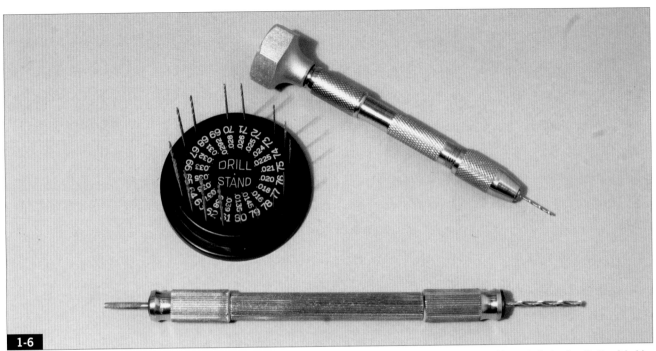

1-6

A pin vise and Nos. 61-80 bits are invaluable tools. Single-ended pin vises are best for general work; a double-ended pin vise (bottom) holds matching drill bits and taps.

100-blade bulk packs. You'll find keeping a knife handle for each blade style to be much handier than swapping blades on a single handle.

Some modelers prefer surgical scalpels. Although more expensive, these have a thinner, harder blade, are extremely sharp, and will hold their edge longer than a hobby knife. You'll also find single-edge razor blades handy for making fine cuts.

Micro-Mark's modeler's detail chisel (No. 82709) is an excellent tool for removing molded-on details. The heavy, angled blade makes it easy to trim details without gouging the locomotive shell. You'll find photos of it in use throughout this book.

Fine-tip tweezers, **1-4**, work well for handling detail parts. Replace them if the ends become bent or dinged (one trip to a concrete floor can be fatal for fine tweezers). Curved-tip tweezers let you reach into tight spaces. Reverse-pressure tweezers (squeezing opens them), are handy for holding parts while working with them.

Fine-tip sprue cutters are an essential tool. They cut small parts from their sprues without requiring much – if any – cleanup, and their cuts are more precise and easily controlled than hobby knife cuts. Larger side-cut-

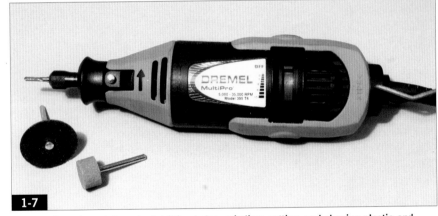

1-7

Motor tools make quick work of drilling holes, grinding, cutting, and shaping plastic and metals.

ters, **1-5**, are good for removing larger molded-on details and for rough trimming on plastic.

A plunger at one end of a screw holder, 1-4, extends prongs out the other end that hold a screw tight while you start it. Use one once and you'll never again start a screw with tweezers, which are just as likely to shoot a screw across the room as hold it securely.

Needlenose and fine-tip pliers, **1-5**, are handy for holding small parts that tweezers can't hold securely.

A pin vise and drill bits are essential for drilling mounting holes for details, **1-6**. Start with a set of Nos. 61-80 bits, along with a few other key sizes

(Nos. 50, 56, and 58, 1/16", 3/32", and 1/8"), then replace them or add other bits as needed. You'll want to keep extras of frequently used bits, especially the common but easily broken No. 80.

A single-chuck pin vise, with a swivel-head, is the easiest to use and the best choice for most modeling work. There are two keys to avoid breaking drill bits: Go slow and drill straight. Apply moderate pressure as you turn the bit, while keeping one finger on the swivel top to keep it aligned. Let the bit do the cutting – don't push to make it cut faster. Once the hole is started, tilting the bit even slightly is an invitation to a broken bit.

1-8

Make a drill bit template by drilling holes around the edge of a thick piece of styrene. This cab sunshade will need a No. 72 mounting hole.

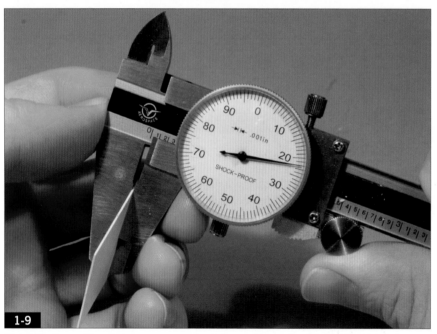

1-9

Dial calipers provide precise measurements of sheet, strip, and rod material and are also good for checking hole depth and clearance dimensions on models.

for various mounting posts, **1-8**. Simply drill a series of holes along the edge of a rectangle of .040" or .060" styrene. Drill a hole for each of your bits, then label them with a permanent marker.

A dial caliper, **1-9**, is the perfect tool for measuring clearances and details on models, including the width and depth of openings and the diameter of round details. Calipers are also handy for checking the diameter and thickness of mounting pegs, wire, and styrene, as well as stray drill bits that always seem to turn up on the workbench.

You'll need a variety of sanding and filing tools to smooth plastic surfaces, **1-10**. I like Squadron's padded sanding sticks, available in several grits. Creations Unlimited offers the similar Flex-I-File sanding sticks. A flexible nail file with multiple grits also works well. Wet/dry sandpaper in 220-, 400-, and 600-grit finishes make quick work of smoothing large surfaces, as does ultra-fine polishing paper such as that from K&S Flex-I-Grit.

Conventional large fine files remove excess material, and jeweler's or needle files are good for cleaning stray material from small castings, smoothing openings, and getting into corners and other hard-to-reach areas.

A self-healing cutting mat is a must for your workbench. These hold work securely and are easy on cutting blades.

A foam cradle, **1-11**, protects your model, especially when you're working on the sides or underbody. You can make one from several pieces of craft foam, or buy a commercial product.

Adhesives

Using the proper adhesive is important for strong bonds between detail parts and locomotive shells, **1-12**. Plastic cements and cyanoacrylates both work well, but it's important to know the jobs each is designed for.

Plastic cement is generally the best choice for plastic-to-plastic joints. The solvent in the glue effectively melts the mating surfaces, welding them. Plastic cement is available in liquid and gel. Liquid cement, sold in small glass jars (often with a brush built in the cap), is usually the handiest. The brush in the jar works for applying cement to broad

Double-ended pin vises keep drill bits with their matching taps (taps are bits that cut screw threads in holes). I keep a double-ended drill/tap for 2-56 screws (No. 50 bit, 2-56 tap) and 1-72 screws (No. 53 bit, 1-72 tap).

You can also drill holes with a motor tool, **1-7**. You'll need one with a chuck that closes completely for fine drill bits, and a dial speed control (or foot pedal) is mandatory for drilling. Even tools that offer several preset speeds generally turn too fast for drilling with small bits.

A motor tool also speeds up grinding and shaping plastic and metal. Various sizes and shapes of router-type bits trim and shape plastic, and grinding stones work for brass and other metals. Other handy accessories include cut-off discs and polishing and sanding pads. When using a motor tool to shape plastic, be sure to use low speed and pause frequently to avoid heat buildup that can quickly cause plastic to melt or deform.

A drill template makes it easy to quickly determine the hole size needed areas, but for fine work, dedicate a fine brush to glue use.

The best way to apply liquid cement is to dip the brush into the liquid and touch it to the joint, allowing capillary action to pull it into the joint. For larger surfaces, you can use a brush to coat the surfaces, then press them together. Gel-type cement is thicker, and is generally sold in plastic bottles with built-in applicator tubes. It's handy for applying directly to mating surfaces, and it's easy to control.

With either type of plastic cement, it's important to have a plastic-to-plastic joint. Don't apply it to a painted surface or the resulting joint will be weak. Scrape the paint off the mating surface or use a cyanoacrylate adhesive.

Cyanoacrylate adhesive (CA) works best for bonding dissimilar materials, such as styrene to metal, and for metal-to-metal joints. Medium-viscosity CA the handiest; it fills small gaps, is easy to control, and has a bit of working time before it sets. Just put a drop or two on a piece of scrap plastic, then apply with a toothpick, wire, or pin.

CA tends to fog clear plastic in enclosed areas as it cures. The best choice for window glazing and other clear styrene items is clear plastic cement. It comes out of the bottle white, but dries clear.

Safety

Most hobby tools aren't considered dangerous, but knives, files, and other tools with sharp edges can easily cause injury. Always wear eye protection when using a motor tool, pin vise, hobby knife, or tweezers. Small drill bits and blade tips break easily, and can fly anywhere – including your face.

Always use proper ventilation when using plastic cement, solvents, putty, and solvent-based paint. Short-term effects of exposure to the solvent vapors in these items include headache and dizziness; long-term exposure can cause serious damage to your central nervous system.

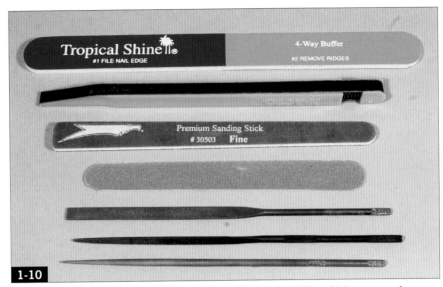

1-10

Common shaping tools include, from top, a flexible padded nail file with four areas of differing coarseness; an X-Acto sanding stick with removable sanding belt; a Squadron flexible sanding stick; a common nail file; and needle files in various shapes.

1-11

A cradle made of soft foam pads is handy for holding locomotives on their sides or upside down.

1-12

Frequently used glues include plastic cements in gel and liquid versions, including Testor's; cyanoacrylate adhesive (CA), such as Insta-Cure medium; and clear parts cement such as Microscale Micro Kristal Klear and Model Master Clear Parts Adhesive.

CHAPTER TWO

Little details, big results

The addition of a few basic detail items turned an ordinary Proto 1000 model into a realistic replication of a Northern Pacific diesel.

Relatively common detail parts can easily enhance the appearance of a decorated model. Many, such as lift rings, m.u. hoses, sunshades, windshield wipers, and grab irons, are essentially generic. They're found on a variety of models regardless of prototype railroad or era. Other details are prototype-specific, and can be purchased as you need them. These include horns, antennas, plows, and headlight castings.

Start with a shave

We'll start by making some basic detail additions to factory-painted diesel models, using as examples a Kato GP35 decorated for the Chicago, Burlington & Quincy, **2-1**, and a Proto 1000 F3 painted in Northern Pacific's freight scheme, **2-2**.

The Kato GP35 was a state-of-the-art model when it came out in the early 1990s, and it is typical of diesel models of that period. Although it doesn't have the level of detail of today's top-of-the-line models, it's still a very good model. Little-used or even new-in-box models of this period are readily available for good prices at swap meets, hobby shops, and online auction sites. These older models should still run well, and many have accurate paint schemes and good basic detailing.

The Proto 1000 model is typical of today's mid-level diesel models, with a smooth-running drive and a paint scheme based on a specific prototype, both of which elevate it above train-set-quality models. The shell itself is decent, but many details are cast in place or omitted.

Both types of models are good candidates for additional details. (The complete list of details I added to each is in **2-5** and **2-6**.) With a bit of extra time and patience, models like this can benefit from the application of more-advanced details, as the following chapters will show. Prototype photos are a great source for planning details for your model. Even in black and white, I found plenty to study in these old photos, **2-3** and **2-5**.

Start by removing the shells from the chassis. This is usually straight-forward, but some models require persistence. Shells may have tabs that snap onto the chassis; some models use screws for mounting; and on

2-1 Fresh from the box, this Kato GP35 runs beautifully and features decent detail and a good paint job. It's typical of high-end diesel models made through the 1990s.

2-2 This Proto 1000 F3 is a plain-Jane model typical of today's mid-price offerings. It runs well, has good paint and lettering, and presents a lot of potential for upgrading.

2-3 Although it's an F7 instead of an F3, 19-year-old Northern Pacific No. 6008D shared many common details with that railroad's F3s, including nose lift rings, winterization hatch, spark arrestors, m.u. hoses, and nail antenna.

2-4 Burlington GP35 No. 980 was brand new when this 1963 photo was taken. It's a sister locomotive to No. 984, which the Kato model represents.

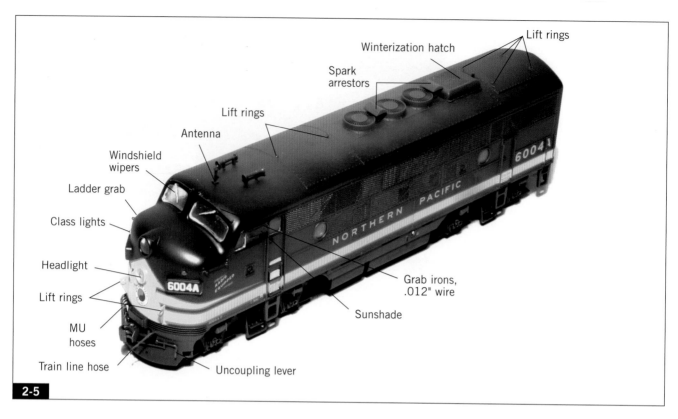

Lift rings

Winterization hatch

Spark arrestors

Lift rings

Antenna

Windshield wipers

Ladder grab

Class lights

Headlight

Lift rings

MU hoses

Train line hose

Uncoupling lever

Grab irons, .012" wire

Sunshade

NORTHERN PACIFIC

6004A

6004

2-5

others, the coupler boxes hold the shells in place. Check the instruction manual or exploded diagram if you have problems. Don't force anything, as a cracked shell can be difficult or impossible to repair.

Before adding new details, fill any holes from factory-applied details that you're removing. On these models, this includes the GP35's original horn

mounting hole on the cab roof and the mounting slot for the drop step on each end platform.

You can use body putty to fill holes, but I find cyanoacrylate adhesive (CA) to be easier to control. Place a drop of CA in the hole, 2-7, with a toothpick, then add a small drop of CA accelerator, such as Zip Kicker, to the CA with a pipette or toothpick. This cures the

CA instantly. Make sure to get the CA in the hole, not just smeared over it.

Shave the area smooth with a hobby knife or detail chisel, then use a sanding stick to further smooth it, 2-8. The tri-grit Squadron stick works well, as you can start with the coarse grit and work to the fine grit until the area is smooth. Chapters 3 and 4 show more examples of filling and hiding holes and gaps. You'll have to use a brush to touch up the area with matching paint – see the sidebar on page 25 for guidelines on paint selection.

Lift rings and grab irons

Grab irons and lift rings are good starter details. You'll learn several skills while installing them, and almost all rolling stock looks better with more-realistic irons and rings. I try to keep the most common types on hand, including ring-style wire eye bolts and 18" grab irons in both standard and drop styles, 2-9.

The Kato model doesn't include lift rings, but it does have starting dimples for drilling at the appropriate locations on the roof, 2-10. This is common on Athearn and other manufacturers' models as well. Adding lift rings is a matter of drilling the dimples with a

---

Parts List: Proto 1000
Northern Pacific F3

A-Line
29211 cab sunshades

Cal-Scale
417 headlight
439 spark arrestors

Detail Associates
1102 nose lift rings
1508 m.u. hoses
1708 class light lenses
2203 nut-bolt-washer castings
2206 eye bolts
2215 ladder grabs
2504 .012" wire (for grab irons)

2805 truck journals, square
2806 truck journals, sloped
2809 brake cylinder piping

Details West
163 winterization hatch
316 uncoupling lever, pilot style
322 antenna, nail type

Kadee
33 coupler (front)
153 coupler (rear)

Precision Scale
3968 windshield wipers

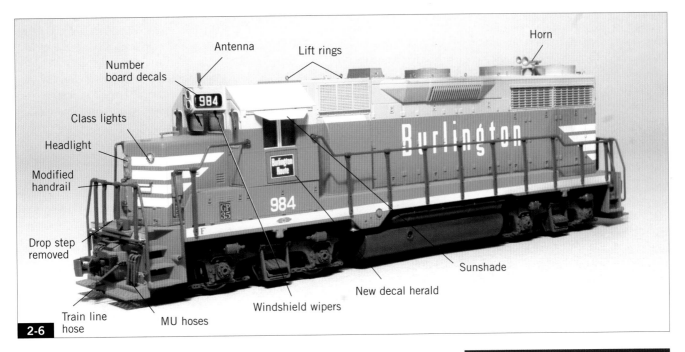

Number board decals
Antenna
Lift rings
Horn
Class lights
Headlight
Modified handrail
Drop step removed
Train line hose
MU hoses
Windshield wipers
New decal herald
Sunshade

2-6

No. 80 bit, then pressing the lift rings into place, **2-11**. You can either dip the stem of the part into a drop of CA before placing it in the hole or use a toothpick to add CA from inside the shell after the part is in place. With lift rings and grab irons, make sure the wires protruding inside the shell don't interfere with the chassis, frame, circuit board, weight, or other internal parts when the body is returned to the chassis. If space is going to be tight, trim the part before adding it.

This style of lift ring is available in wire, cast brass, and plastic from several detail makers. I prefer the wire ones, which have a fine cross section and are strong – an important consideration on the roof where you're likely to handle

the model. Cast metal pieces appear heavier, and plastic versions are prone to breaking. In fact, it's not a bad idea to replace factory-installed plastic lift rings with wire ones.

The Proto 1000 model has molded-on bumps at the lift-ring locations. Carefully trim these off with a sprue nipper, hobby knife, or detail chisel, **2-12**. Remove as little paint as possible and make sure the area is smooth. Mark the center of the shaved-off area with a pin to provide a starting mark for the bit and drill the hole. Add the lift ring and touch up the ring and surrounding area as needed with a fine-point brush.

The Kato model had separate grab irons molded in engineering plastic. I

Parts List: Chicago, Burlington & Quincy GP35

A-Line
29200 windshield wipers
29210 sunshades

Detail Associates
1003 headlight (nose)
1508 m.u. hoses
2508 .028" wire (handrail)

Kadee
5 couplers

MV Products
300 lenses, classification lights

Microscale
87-15 CB&Q hood unit decals (heralds)
87-48 decals (builder's plates)
87-527 diesel detail decals (class light gaskets)

Precision Scale
39133 antenna, firecracker type

ShellScale
105 number board decals

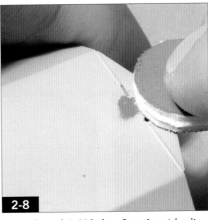

2-7

2-8

Place a drop of CA in the old mounting hole with a toothpick, then add a drop of accelerator to cure the CA.

A sanding stick (this is a Squadron tri-grit flexible stick) sands the area smooth.

decided to keep them, but swapping them for finer metal parts is an option taken by many modelers – see chapters 3 and 4 for details.

The Northern Pacific F unit needed a ladder-hook grab on each side of the nose, **2-13**. Locate the mounting hole locations following prototype photos. Make sure the holes are level, then drill with a pin vise. Nut-bolt-washer (NBW) castings are optional, but they're nice extra details and make the grab look like it's bolted in place like the real thing. Drill mounting holes for these about one drill-bit-width away from the iron mounting hole (above or below as appropriate).

Templates are handy for frequently used parts, **2-14**. I have them for standard and ladder grabs of various lengths, with locating holes for both the grab iron and NBW castings. To use them, make sure the template is properly and securely positioned, then mark the hole locations with a pin.

Many cab units eventually received what are known as "eyebrow" grab irons above the cab windows, **2-14**, as well as long grabs above the side cab windows and doors. These are easy to make using .012" wire, **2-15**. Bend them to length following photos, then drill holes and glue them in place.

Headlights

A headlight is a small detail part, but it's an important focal point on a locomotive. Headlights come in many different styles. Diesel model manufacturers can't duplicate all of these variations, but fortunately the detail makers offer accurate renditions of headlights made by Mars, Pyle, and others.

Check prototype photos and modeling articles to determine the proper headlights for your models. Also, keep in mind that these items sometimes changed through the life of a locomotive.

Headlights on hood units like this Burlington are generally centered above the cab, and some are found on the nose as well. These nose lights often differ in style from the main headlight, with one set being a standard headlight and the other a warning or other type of light.

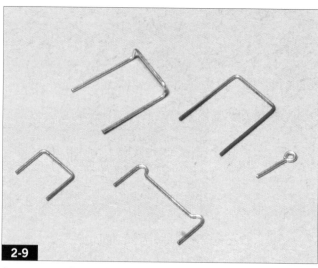

2-9 Common parts (clockwise from top left) include 18" drop and straight grab irons, lift rings, ladder grabs, and narrow (14") grabs.

2-10 Following the locating dimples, use a pin vise to drill No. 80 holes for the rooftop lift rings.

2-11 Use tweezers to press the new wire lift rings into place.

2-12 Some models have bumps instead of lift rings. Shave these off with a detail chisel.

Chapter 3 shows how to remove molded headlight details and replace them with separate details. Some headlight installations require a different approach. As an example, the Burlington equipped its hood units with nose-mounted headlights, a feature lacking on the Kato model. Trim the new part from its sprue and remove any mold flash or stray sprue marks.

To add this detail, begin carving the nose with a hobby knife to match the notch on the prototype. Work slowly and check the fit of the headlight casting until it fits properly. Use liquid plastic cement to glue the new headlight casting in place, **2-17**.

Use a brush to paint the casting and carved area the proper color – Modelflex CB&Q Chinese Red was the best match in this case.

If the lenses won't be lighted (as with the above-cab lenses on the GP35), you can use silver-backed lenses as made by MV Products and others. These rest in the recesses of the headlight casting and don't require drilling through the casting or shell.

To add these lenses, place a drop of CA in the recess of the headlight casting. They're difficult to handle – tweezers are likely to shoot them across your workshop. Instead, make a handling stick by dipping the end of a toothpick in rubber cement, **2-18**. Let it dry for a few minutes until tacky. This makes it easy to pick up the lens by its face and place it precisely in the casting.

To illuminate a headlight, drill a hole through the casting and shell, **2-19**, and add a clear lens to the open-

2-13

New nose details include a ladder grab with nut-bolt-washer (NBW) castings above it, grabs and NBW castings above the windshields, class-light lenses, lift rings, and a new lower headlight.

ing. Make sure the bit matches the size of your lens and is no wider than the inside of the circular brackets for the lens.

You may be able to use the lenses that come with the locomotive, but sometimes they won't match the size of the replacement casting. Commercial lenses are made by Detail Associates and others (see the following section on classification lights for an example).

You can also make your own lenses to precisely fit any headlight casting. Although it might be considered a more-advanced project, turning a clear

lens isn't that difficult if you own a drill press or power hand drill.

Start with a length of clear plastic. You can find commercial plastic rod, or use a piece of clear plastic sprue left over from a kit as I did. Chuck the clear plastic in the drill press (or in a power drill held firmly in a vise). Shape the rod on a mill file, **2-20**, at low speed. Remove material gradually – working too fast, or at a speed too high, will melt the plastic. Check the diameter frequently with a caliper or micrometer, or by checking it with the mounting hole, **2-21**.

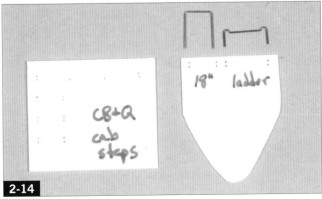

2-14

Styrene templates with holes for common grab irons make it easy to mark mounting locations on models.

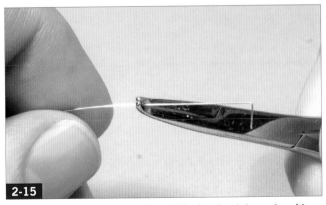

2-15

It's easy to make grab irons using .012" wire. Bend the grabs with small pliers.

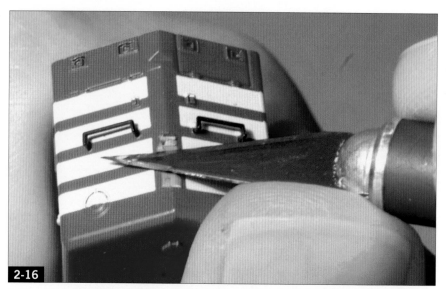

2-16

Carve a notch for the new headlight with a hobby knife. Be sure the area is flat across the nose.

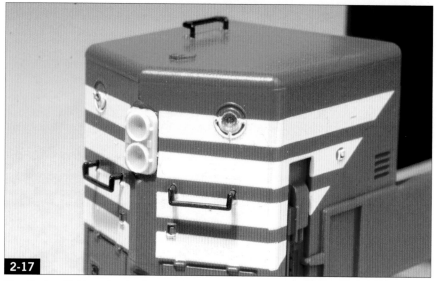

2-17

Glue the headlight casting in place on the notch. The class light at left has been marked in the center for drilling; the one at right has been drilled deep enough to hold an MV lens.

Once the lens is the proper diameter, cut it to length. File the lens end flat, and use a fine sanding stick to polish it smooth. Place the lens in the opening and secure it with liquid plastic cement added from behind the shell. Applying a drop of clear gloss finish to the lens surface will give it a glass-like appearance. If you decide you want a working light, chapter 4 has more information about illuminating a headlight.

The F unit presented another challenge. The model has a single headlight, but prototype NP F units had dual headlights. Precision Scale offers a brass casting for a lower headlight,

2-22. Add the lower headlight in the nose door by drilling a hole centered at the top of the door to fit the rear of the casting.

Glue the new casting in place with CA. Because the nose is curved, the casting will create edge gaps between the casting and nose door. Fill these with CA applied with a toothpick carved to a chisel point, **2-23.** Work slowly, using just enough CA to fill the gap.

Once the glue dries, touch up the casting with the proper color – in this case Modelflex NP Yellow. If installed properly, the casting will look molded on.

You can use a commercial lens in the casting, but you might want to learn another handy technique using clear epoxy. If the headlight casting has an opening at the rear, as this one does, glue a disc of clear styrene across the hole, or glue a small lens in the opening. Stand the shell on its end, propping it securely, and paint the inside of the casting (the lens area) silver.

Mix a small batch of five-minute epoxy on a scrap piece of plastic. Apply it with a toothpick, placing it drop-by-drop to avoid over-filling the cupped area, **2-24.** The epoxy will level nicely and dry clear. The headlight can be lit from behind if desired.

Classification lights

Until a few decades ago, locomotives ran with classification lights, the small lights on either side of the nose. White lights indicated the train was an extra section; green lights meant another section of the train followed. The lights were illuminated primarily at night, with flags used in daylight. The use of class lights varied among railroads, and diminished into the 1970s as more railroads switched from timetable-and-train-order operation to other control systems. By the 1980s, class lights had been removed from many diesels and their positions were plated over.

Some newer models have clear lenses in their class-light housings, while other models (including the F3 and GP35 here) simply have them molded into the shell. You can upgrade these using different types of lights.

Adding non-illuminated lenses, such as those from MV, is simple. As shown on the Kato model, start by marking the center of the molded "lens" bump with a pin. Using a bit to match the diameter of the lens, drill just deep enough for the lens to sit.

I used a fine brush to paint the body color in the area between the notch and the molded gasket, **2-25,** where the white striping had intruded. I added the black gaskets using decals from Microscale set No. 87-527. More information on applying decals can be found in chapter 5. Glue the lens in place using the same techniques as with the headlights shown earlier.

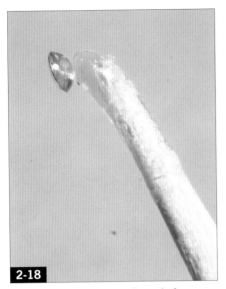

2-18

A bit of rubber cement on the end of a toothpick works well for holding MV lenses.

2-19

To illuminate a headlight, slowly drill a hole through the casting and shell. The class light lenses and gasket decals are in place.

You can also install lenses that pass through the shell. These can be illuminated or non-illuminated lenses, but if you don't want them to light up, paint the back of the lens silver. To add these lenses as I did on the F unit, drill the appropriate hole centered on the molded lens bump. Press the new lens in place, **2-26**, and glue it from behind with liquid plastic cement.

Hoses and pilot details

Multiple-unit (m.u.) hoses and cables can be found on most hood and cab diesels. Depending upon the era and brake system, a locomotive might have three, four, or five hoses on each side of the coupler, along with the heavier train line hose to the right of the coupler (as you're looking at the end of the diesel). Check prototype photos for specifics for your models.

I always keep a supply of Detail Associates m.u. hoses handy, as well as Cal-Scale train line hoses. These can be applied individually to match specific prototypes. Details West and others make metal castings for groups of hoses that can be applied as a single item. These also work well, and chapter 4 shows an example.

Some models (such as the Kato GP35) include drilling dimples as a guide; for others, you're on your own. Mark the hose locations with a pin based on photos. Drill mounting holes, then glue the hoses in

2-20

Turn a headlight lens by chucking clear plastic rod in a drill press and filing it to size.

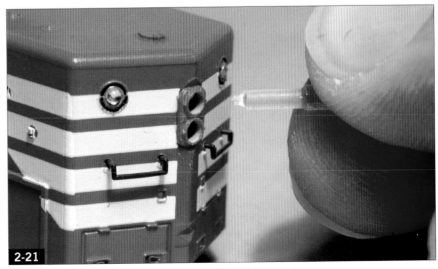

2-21

Once the clear rod fits, trim the end flat and glue it in the opening.

place with CA. It's often easier to paint hoses before installation: Grimy black works well for the hoses themselves, with medium to dark gray for the glad hands (connectors) and hardware.

The train line hose is a separate item and will be on all diesels regardless of whether they have m.u. connections. Again, drill a mounting hole and glue the part in place.

Some modelers prefer to omit this item, letting the metal uncoupling pin on the coupler serve as the train line, but for a better appearance, I like to add the hose and cut off the uncoupling pins on my diesel models. (More on that in chapter 6.)

Many F units and other cab diesels only had m.u. connections on the rear (at both ends of B units); others had connections on the nose as well, or had connections added after the locomotive was in service. The NP Fs had five hoses on each side, mounted in the anticlimber. Some railroads removed the hoses when the locomotives were leading; the NP F in the photos only had the hoses in place on one side. Again, use prototype photos as a guide.

Uncoupling levers are visible details on pilots. On hood units, these come in a couple of basic styles, but feature a bar that goes across the pilot, held by several mounting brackets. Some models (especially early ones) have these

molded in place; others have separate items, which range in realism from good to poor.

I decided to keep the stock uncoupling lever on the Kato model, but chapters 3 and 4 show how to add two styles of wire levers with brackets.

Cab units had a different style of lever that followed the curve of the pilot. Depending upon the pilot style, the lever might be located behind the pilot, with only the handle visible at the side. The NP model features the most common style found on open-type "freight" pilots. I had a spare InterMountain plastic lever. Details West also offers a metal casting that's quite realistic.

Test-fit the new lower headlight in its mounting hole, then glue it in place with CA.

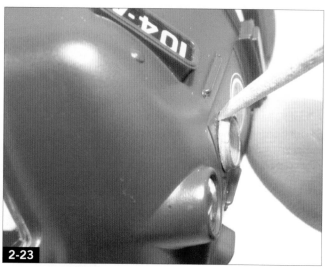

Use a toothpick carved with a chisel tip to add CA to the gap between the headlight casting and shell. Work slowly and go around the entire diameter of the headlight.

Add epoxy drop by drop to the headlight casting. Although not shown here, it's a good idea to cover surrounding areas with masking tape to avoid getting stray epoxy on the shell.

Paint out the white stripe with body color inside the class-light casting.

Paint these items as appropriate. They often match the body; but some railroads painted them in contrasting colors.

Windshields

Most models today come with form-fitting clear plastic glazing that rests flush in the window openings. The windshields and windows in these models fit reasonably well, but the windshields of both models in this chapter had molded-in wiper detail, which I think detracts from the models' appearance. So my next detail improvement was adding separate wipers.

Since the windows themselves fit well, I wanted to save them, which meant removing the molded-in detail. Start with a detail chisel or knife to shave off the cast-in wipers, **2-27**. Be careful not to cut into the surface.

Sand the clear plastic, beginning with 400-grit sandpaper and progressing through several grades to 1000-grit polishing paper. You can also use a multi-grit sanding stick such as the Squadron No. 30505, **2-28**. Use the coarser grit to remove any marks from the cutting tool. Once they're gone, keep moving to the next-finer grit, using a circular pattern. Finish with the polishing surface until the window is again glossy.

A couple applications of liquid plastic polish, **2-29**, will enhance the finish. With a soft cloth, rub the liquid onto the surface in a circular pattern. Start with the heavy scratch remover, then move to the fine scratch remover.

Some older models have pieces of clear plastic that simply rest behind the window openings, revealing the thick styrene walls of the body. The best way to improve the appearance of these is to replace them with laser-cut press-in windows, available for many models (shown in chapter 3), or by cutting your own windows from clear styrene sheet, as shown in chapter 4.

Handrails

A common hood unit detail variation is the end handrail. Some railroads equip their locomotives with drop steps on the end platforms, enabling crew members to walk between engines

2-26 Drill a mounting hole for the class light using the model's bump as a guide, then glue the lens in place.

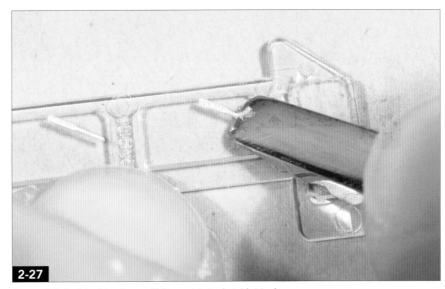

2-27 Use a detail chisel to shave off the molded windshield wipers.

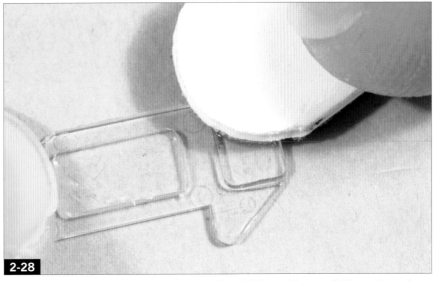

2-28 Sand the glazing with progressively finer abrasive, finishing with the polishing surface of a sanding stick.

2-29

Liquid scratch removers, such as Novus, work well for polishing clear styrene.

while the train is in motion. Locomotives with these have a gap in the end railing, with a chain across the gap (the chains are connected between adjoining locomotives when coupled). Locomotives without drop steps have solid end handrails with no gap.

Some models today come in a choice of versions based on specific prototypes. However the older Kato model came only in drop steps, whereas the real Burlington GP35s didn't use them. The Kato GP35 has engineering-plastic handrails, so converting them was a challenge because this material can't be glued easily.

Start with a sprue trimmer to remove the drop step, which is molded to the stanchions. Clean up the cut lines as needed with a knife. Cut away the molded "chain" between the middle stanchions, **2-30**, leaving the cut area as flat as possible.

I replaced the chain with a piece of Detail Associates .028" wire, which even though slightly oversize, most closely matched the diameter of the molded handrail.

To give the wire a secure place to rest, drill out each side of the molded stanchion top, **2-31**, with a No. 70 bit. This takes some precision and care. Having a flat area to work with helps, followed by a starting point marked with a pin.

Make this point as close to the center of the stanchion top as possible. Drill into the molding a scale 4" or

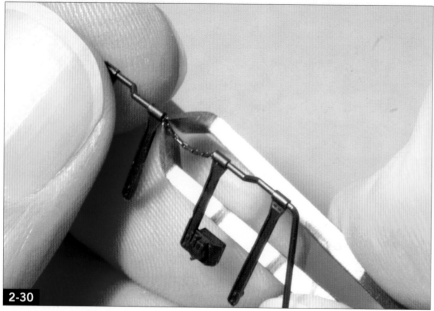

2-30

Cut away the molded plastic chain using sprue nippers. Trim as close to the stanchion as possible.

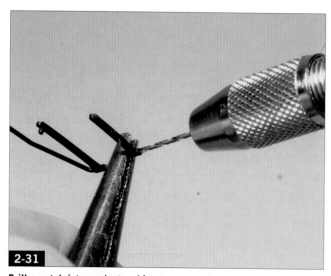

2-31

Drill a notch into each stanchion to accept the new end handrail.

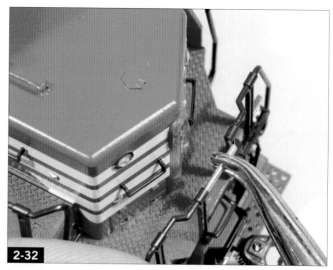

2-32

Press the new end handrail into the notches drilled into each stanchion.

so – deep enough to give the new wire a snug fit.

Place each half of the end handrail/ stanchion assemblies in place on the platform, making sure the stanchions are vertical. Cut the new wire piece slightly longer than the gap and test-fit it, **2-32**. Dip each end in CA, then use needle-nose pliers to place it, **2-33**. Paint it to match the rest of the handrail assembly.

Roof

Many diesels operating in cold areas have winterization hatches applied over one or more radiator fans. These boxes with shutters and screen openings can capture warm air expelled by the radiator fan and redirect it to the engine room.

The NP F needed a winterization hatch on its rear-most radiator fan. Adding a Details West plastic casting required first carving away much of the shell's high-profile fan housing, **2-34**. I then test-fitted the detail part, **2-35**, and glued it in place.

The F unit also needed spark arrestors, which were added to the exhaust stacks of many non-turbocharged EMD diesels – mainly early Geeps, F and E units, and switchers. They came in several styles.

Spark arrestor installation varies depending upon the style. Many, including the Cal-Scale details on this model, have the exhaust stacks cast with the spark arrestors. This means

2-33

The new handrail blends with the original. Paint it black to match.

removing the shell's original stacks, **2-34**. Test-fit the arrestors, then glue them and the new winterization hatch in place with CA.

Fan detail varies greatly among models. Many new models have excellent parts, with separate grills and fan blades, **2-36**. Others, such as the NP F, are much simpler, simply having the outer grill detail, with the entire fan housing, integral with the body shell.

The Kato model is in the middle, with the fans molded into the shell, but with a good rendition of the effect of separate grill and blade detail, **2-37**. Some modelers choose to replace these with separate fans from Cannon & Co., Detail Associates, Smokey Valley,

and others. However, with a bit of time and paint, it's possible to enhance fans with molded-in blade detail to give them a more-realistic look.

Start by painting the blades silver or light gray (I used silver on the Kato model, since the roof was already painted light gray), **2-37**, with a fine brush. Follow this by painting the top of each grill black or grimy black, **2-38** Don't use regular brush strokes – instead, pat the side of the brush on the grill itself so that only the top of the grill receives any paint.

The contrast in colors looks quite realistic, **2-39**, making the blades and grills look like separate items. You can enhance the look further by adding

2-34

The exhaust stacks need to be carefully carved away, and the rear-most fan must be shortened while the front of it is trimmed for the new winterization hatch.

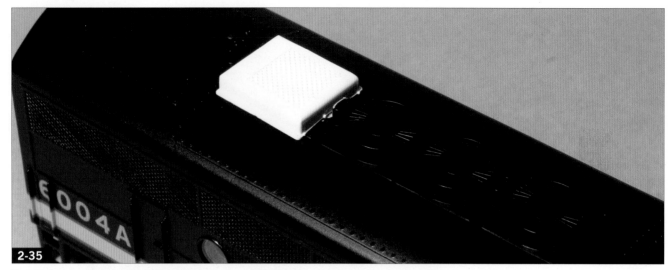

2-35

Test-fit the new winterization hatch as you trim the radiator fan.

2-36

Some newer models, such as the Atlas SD35, have outstanding fan detail with separate grills and blades.

2-37

Begin upgrading molded fan detail by using a fine brush to paint the individual blades silver.

a black wash between the fan blades. Chapter 5 shows examples of this.

Trucks

Although many modelers overlook them, truck sideframes offer opportunities for detail upgrades. Individual truck designs evolved over the years, with changing journal covers, speed-recorder cables (see chapter 4), sand lines (see chapter 4), brake shoes (see chapter 3), and shock dampers.

As an example, the journal covers on the F unit model differed from those on the real thing, and changing them is not difficult. Early trucks had several styles of journal covers, including the style molded into the Proto 1000 models as well as larger square and sloped-top versions.

Detail Associates offers both the square and sloped style covers, both of which are found on the NP F: The rear sideframe has one sloped and one square, while the forward sideframe has two square covers.

Start by shaving off the existing journal covers with a hobby knife. Use a flat needle file to even up the area, **2-40**. The needle file also roughens up the mating surfaces, important because glue doesn't stick well to smooth acetal plastic.

Apply CA to the area with a toothpick, then place the new journal covers, **2-41**. The CA will hold the covers reasonably well, but avoid handling them.

An easily added detail on EMD's four-wheel GP truck (often called a

Blomberg truck) is the air line between the brake cylinders. Detail Associates offers pre-shaped wire for this; you can also bend your own .012" wire. Either way, to add this detail, drill No. 80 holes in the end of each brake cylinder, **2-42**. Slip each end of the wire into the cylinders, applying a small drop of CA to hold them in place, and paint them black. A before-and-after view of the F unit sideframe can be seen in **2-43**.

Final details

Horns vary greatly by era and railroad, and fortunately for modelers, manufacturers offer a variety of plastic and brass castings based on real horns. To determine the proper horn type and placement, check prototype photos, information in magazine articles, or on the internet. An excellent Web site (atsf.railfan.net/airhorns) is devoted to the subject.

For the NP F unit, I kept the stock horns that came with the model, which was the most-common arrangement on real F units. On the Kato model, the horn needed to be moved from the cab roof to the rear of the long hood to match the CB&Q prototype. The stock horn that came with the model resembles the real Burlington horn, but the CB&Q horn had two trumpets instead of three, both facing forward. Modifying this horn was easy. A nipper to removed the rearward-facing middle bell, **2-44**, and a knife cleaned up the area.

I added a new extended mounting post by drilling a No. 70 hole in the bottom of the horn casting and gluing a piece of .028" wire into the hole, **2-45**. Drill a matching hole at the appropriate spot (in this case just ahead of the small radiator fan on the left side of the roof), then glue it in place with CA.

Antennas are another detail that vary widely. Adding these details is generally simple: Just drill a mounting hole and glue the detail in place. Antennas are generally known by their maker or by their shape; the NP unit received a brass "nail" antenna, and the CB&Q model got a "firecracker" type.

The Northern Pacific equipped its F units with distinctive nose-mounted

2-38 Use the side of a brush to dab paint on the top of the grill, being careful not to get paint on the blades.

2-39 The contrast in colors among the blades, grill, and body makes the fans look like separate details.

2-40 Remove the existing journal covers with a knife, then file the areas flat with a needle file.

2-41

Glue the new journal covers in place with CA. This sideframe uses one square (left) and one angled cover.

2-42

To add an air line, drill the end of each brake cylinder with a No. 80 bit.

2-43

The stock Proto 1000 sideframe is at top; the bottom one has new journals and an air line between brake cylinders.

lift rings. Adding the new styrene Detail Associates items was mostly a matter of carefully scraping the paint away at the proper locations on the nose to provide a good bonding surface, then using plastic cement to glue the new parts in place. A bit of paint blended lift rings into the nose.

Windshield wipers are another distinctive detail that's easy to add, requiring just a mounting hole above the windshield for mounting. A-Line, Detail Associates, and Precision Scale all offer several styles of wipers, all sharply molded in plastic. Check prototype photos when painting, as some

have the shafts painted to match the locomotive; others are metallic gray or grimy black.

Sunshades are common on many diesels. Since they protrude from the model, durability is important, making A-Line's brass offerings a good choice. A-Line offers two styles, one designed for cab units and one for hood units. Paint them before cutting them from their sprues. Drill matching holes on the model using the holes on the brass sprues as a guide, then add them to the model, **2-46**. The brass mounting tabs can be bent over on the inside to secure the pieces.

The Kato model has a simplified cab, with seats and a rough control stand. With glazing in place, it's difficult to see fine detail in a cab, but adding a figure, **2-47**, is an easy way to upgrade the appearance. Preiser and others make a variety of seated figures.

The lettering on newer models is generally quite good, but occasionally you'll find something that can be added or upgraded. I added builder's plate decals to the GP35 and replaced the Burlington Route herald on the cab with a more-accurate decal as described in chapter 5.

None of the alterations described here require a tremendous amount of work, but all add greatly to the appearance and realism of the models. All that's left is to add some weathering as chapter 5 describes and the models are ready for the layout, **2-48**.

Now let's look at making some more extensive detail upgrades to other models.

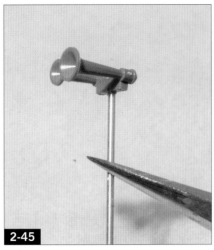

2-44

Trimming the middle trumpet from the Kato horn made it more closely match the real CB&Q horn.

2-45

The new mounting post of .028" wire fits into a hole drilled into the horn casting.

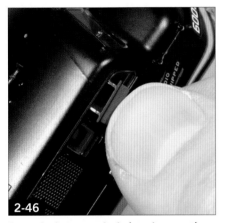

2-46

Press the brass sunshade into the mounting holes, then bend the brass tabs over inside the shell.

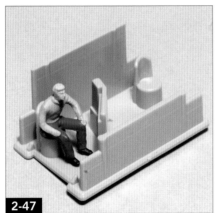

2-47

Gluing a seated Preiser figure in the cab helps improve the interior's appearance.

Matching touch-up paint

When adding details to decorated models you'll need to paint the details to match the model, and you'll need to touch up any areas on the model that have been sanded or filled.

Unfortunately there's no magic formula or technique to matching paint – it's a hit-or-miss process that requires testing paints until you find a close enough color. You can add a bit of white or black to model paint to change the shade, but it's difficult to blend multiple colors to come up with a third color. That's because model paints are already blends of other colors.

The good news is that you generally don't need an exact match. Getting a color in the ballpark is usually good enough for small details such as lift rings and grab irons, and a bit of weathering will hide differences in larger areas. With the hundreds of available model colors (don't forget automotive and military colors), it's almost always possible to come very close with color.

2-48

The completed Burlington GP35 is ready to go to work hauling freight trains on a layout.

CHAPTER THREE

Beyond the basics

This Rio Grande GP40-2 started out as a stock Athearn model. Extensive detailing on the body, pilots, and underbody brought it closer to the appearance of a real D&RGW diesel.

The basic details we added in the last chapter are the first steps in creating more-prototypical locomotives. You can take your models from good to great with just a little more cutting, drilling, filing, and fitting.

3-1

Here's the Great Northern RS-2 as it comes from the manufacturer. The paint and lettering are accurate, but the model lacks many separate detail items.

Upgrade, don't replace

Customizing a contemporary model like the Proto 1000 Great Northern Alco RS-2 and an older Athearn Rio Grande GP40-2 will be great practice. The GN model, **3-1**, like the Northern Pacific F in chapter 3, has a paint scheme that matches its prototype, but it's a bare-bones model. The shell itself has no grab irons and a limited number of separate details. The prototype GN's RS-2s, **3-2**, had many distinctive features including steam-style marker lights and number boxes as well as roof access ladders on the hood.

The Rio Grande locomotive is an older Athearn model from the 1990s. I had added some basic details and weathering to it several years ago, **3-3**. It's typical of the many older – but still good – used models that can be found at affordable prices. Perhaps you have a similar model or two running on your layout that doesn't quite match the detail level of new models on the market. Instead of replacing them with new models, you can upgrade them to today's standards with some details and a bit of work.

The complete detail lists for the models can be seen in **3-4** and **3-5**.

Number boards and markers

The GN's RS-2s, like the railroad's other early hood diesels, were set up

3-2

The real Great Northern No. 201, shown here in 1959, has several interesting variations uncommon for RS-2s, including full-height ladders, angled number boards, steam-style class lights, and a bracket-style bell on the roof.

3-3

When purchased in the 1990s, this Athearn model had received a minimum of detail extras, including a plow, horn, grab irons, and number board decals, with a bit of weathering.

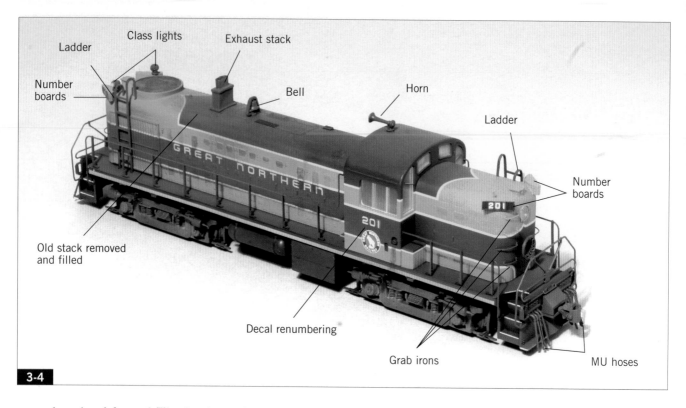

Ladder — Class lights — Exhaust stack — Bell — Horn — Ladder — Number boards — Number boards — Old stack removed and filled — Decal renumbering — Grab irons — MU hoses

3-4

to run long-hood forward. The diesels had distinctively shaped number boxes cut into the body at the corners of both the long and short hoods. Detail Associates offers the parts, but adding them requires some carving on the shell.

Start by trimming the model's stock number boards flush with the shell, **3-6**, using a knife and detail chisel to remove as much of the number board as possible. Clean the area with a flexible sanding stick, **3-7**, applying progressively finer grit until it's smooth.

Mark the level of the bottom of the new number boards at each corner a scale 6'-6" above the walkway, **3-8**. Use a hobby knife to start a horizontal cut,

then follow by shaving downward to match the first cut, **3-9**. Trim the material a little bit at a time, working slowly to keep the cut level.

As the cut proceeds through the shell, begin curving the rear of the notch to match the rear of the number board, **3-10**. This is a freehand process, so go slowly and stop when the number board fits into the notch. Make sure the number board is level when the face is at a 45-degree angle.

Glue the number board into the notch with liquid plastic cement, **3-11**.

Parts List: Proto 1000 Great Northern RS-2

Cal-Scale
280 marker lights
322 bell

Custom Finishing
269 extended turbo stack

Detail Associates
1508 m.u. hoses
2602 number boards

Microscale
87-815 Great Northern decals
87-123-1 Number set, white block Gothic (number boards)

MV Products
300 lenses (class lights)

Precision Scale
31327 ladder stock
39083 horn

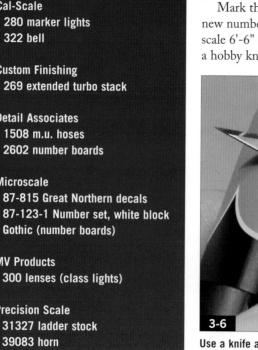

3-6
Use a knife and chisel to trim away the model's stock number boards.

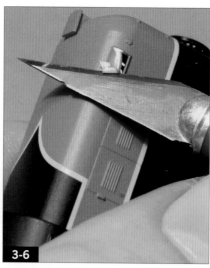

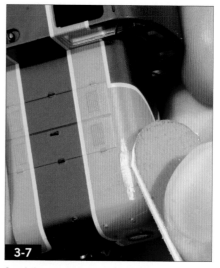

3-7
Sand the number board areas flush with the body.

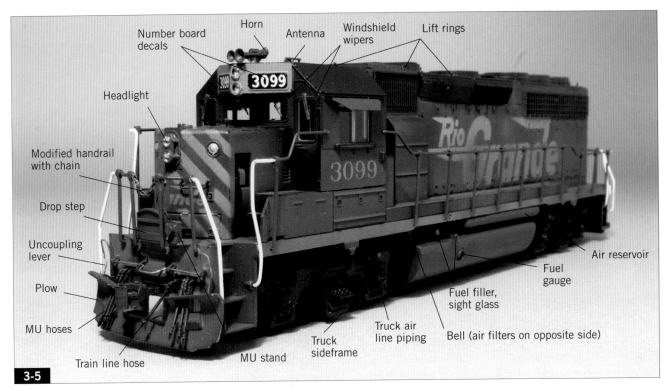

Number board decals — Horn — Antenna — Windshield wipers — Lift rings

Headlight

Modified handrail with chain

Drop step

Uncoupling lever

Plow

MU hoses

Train line hose

MU stand

Truck sideframe

Truck air line piping

Fuel filler, sight glass

Bell (air filters on opposite side)

Fuel gauge

Air reservoir

3099

3-5

Once that dries, fill any gaps between the rear of the number board and the shell with CA. Repeat the process at each corner.

The number board includes etched-brass pieces for the five-digit frame on the number board face, **3-12**. They come in the package attached to a piece of flexible rubber. To get the etched pieces free, soak them for a few minutes in a bottle of lacquer thinner. The solvent will free the parts. Pull them from the bottle with tweezers and dry them on a paper towel.

Two Rio Grande GP40-2s lead their train out of Salt Lake City in September 1983.

Parts list:
Athearn Denver & Rio Grande Western GP40-2

Athearn
42009 truck sideframes

A-Line
29200 windshield wipers
29210 sunshades
29222 chain

American Model Builders
230 window glazing

Cal-Scale
276 train line hoses

Detail Associates
1402 drop step
1505 m.u. stand (late, low)
1508 m.u. hoses
1803 antenna, Sinclair
2202 grab irons
2205 uncoupling lever, AAR Type 1
2206 eye bolts
2809 brake cylinder piping
3101 fuel gauge
3102 fuel tank details
3203 air reservoirs, 15" side
2505 .015" wire

Details West
127 bell
290 headlight, Mars (nose)
139 air filter set
155 plow
186 horn, Nathan M3

MV Products
18 lenses (nose)

ShellScale
117 number board decals

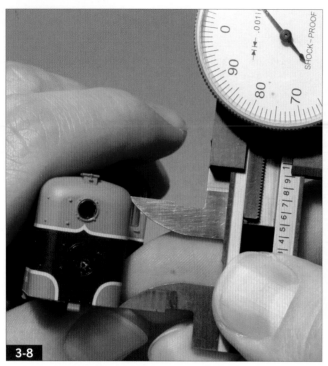

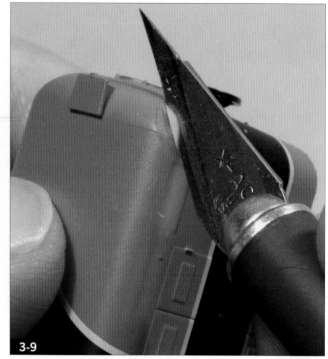

3-8

Mark the height of the bottom of the new number boards at each corner.

3-9

Gradually cut the notch into the body with a hobby knife. Be sure to keep the base cut horizontal.

Use a pin to place a thin line of CA around the edge of the face of the number board, then carefully position the brass frame and press it in place. Paint the number board face black.

Exhaust stack

The Proto 1000 model represents an as-delivered RS-2 with an air-cooled turbocharger. This can be identified by the rectangular exhaust stack positioned lengthwise to the hood and off center. Because of problems with this turbocharger, most RS-2s soon were refitted with water-cooled units. As part of the conversion, the exhaust stack was relocated closer to the cab and turned perpendicular to the hood.

The model's exhaust stack is molded with the shell, so modeling this variation requires first cutting off the original stack. Start by cutting the stack off with side cutters, then trim the remainder of the stack down to roof level with a knife and chisel. The stack is molded with a hole in the middle, so the result is a hole in the roof. The stack is at the

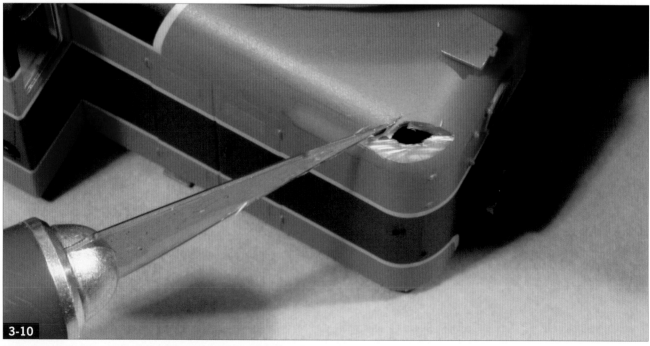

3-10

Curve the back of the notch to match the rear of the number board.

Body putty

Body putty is a popular material for filling gaps, dings, and scratches in plastic models. Common putties include Squadron Green, Squadron White, and Dr. Microtools Red. Always use putty in a well-ventilated area, as putty contains toluene and other hazardous solvents.

Start by using a toothpick or pin to place putty in the indentation or gap. Be sure the putty is fresh: It should be shiny and gooey and should stick readily to the surface.

If you're applying small amounts with a toothpick and if the putty is exposed to the air for too long, it can dry before you get it on the model and will not stick well to the surface.

If you're filling a hole, be sure you get the putty into the hole, not just over it. Don't try to fill a deep crevice or indentation at once or the putty won't dry properly. Instead, build the putty in multiple layers, letting the putty dry completely between coats – a time that can vary by the putty and thickness of the application.

A better idea for large gaps is to use CA (as described in the text) or cut a piece of styrene to fill the main gap. Use progressively coarser sandpaper (or sanding sticks) to remove excess putty and smooth the area, starting with 220 grit and moving to 400-, 600-, and 800-grit. Wet-sanding will provide a smoother surface. If marks remain, apply another coat of putty to that spot and repeat the process.

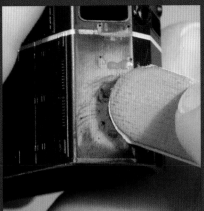

Replacing cast-on details

The photos show putty being applied to an Atlas shell where molded-on grab irons were shaved off to make way for separate details. Many older models have grabs molded in place. Although separate items look better, it can be difficult to remove molded grabs from decorated models without having to repaint large areas.

Use a detail chisel to remove the molded details. Use the marks from the molded details as a guide in drilling mounting holes for the new parts. Fill any gaps with putty or CA, sand the area smooth, then repaint the area. Add the new details as on any other model.

edge of a roof panel, with lots of rivets nearby, so try not to damage the rivets.

Modelers have developed many techniques for filling holes and gaps in plastic shells, but I've become a big fan of using CA and accelerator so that's what I'll describe here. We'll start by gluing a piece of styrene behind the hole inside the shell.

Place a few drops of CA in the gap around the styrene, then use a pipette to apply a drop of CA accelerator to the CA, **3-13**. This will cure the glue instantly. Wipe away any stray accelerator with a paper towel, then repeat the process until the gap is filled.

I prefer CA to body putty (see the sidebar above) because you can work the filled area immediately. CA is workable with standard hobby tools, and dries as hard as the shell itself.

A couple of cautions: Apply accelerator with a pipette, not the spray bottle it comes in. This provides better con-

3-11

Glue the number boards in place at a 45-degree angle. Fill any gaps at the rear with CA.

3-12

Glue the etched-brass frames to the faces of the number boards. This view also shows the grab irons in place.

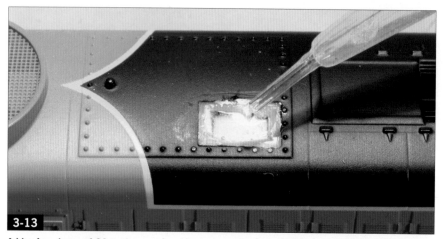

3-13

Add a few drops of CA to the opening, then use a pipette to add CA accelerator. Repeat the process until the gap is filled.

3-14

A flat needle file shapes the CA to match the roofline.

trol, important because accelerator can etch or dissolve some acrylic paints. It's best to apply CA with a toothpick, pin, or wire. It gives the best control, and avoids the risk of accidentally curing an entire bottle of CA by touching the bottle tip to some accelerator left in the gap. Also, do any carving and sanding immediately after the CA has cured. After an hour or so, the CA becomes noticeably harder, making it more difficult to work with.

Shape the CA with a knife, then a small file, **3-14**, and smooth with sanding stick. If any small gaps show up, fill with more CA, a touch more of accelerator, and re-sand.

You're bound to damage some rivets in this process. I replaced several along the edge by shaving off the damaged ones, marking the locations with a pin, then drilling a mounting hole and adding a nut-bolt-washer (NBW) casting with the tops trimmed to match the shape of the body rivets, **3-15**.

The new exhaust stack is a brass detail from Custom Finishing. As with many brass castings, this one required some clean up of molding lines, flash, and irregular edges, **3-16**, which I worked with needle files before adding to the model.

Glue the new exhaust stack in place with CA. It should be centered on the hood on the same original access panel it was on, at the cab edge, **3-17**. Fill any gaps between the exhaust stack base and the hood with CA.

Ladders

The GN's RS-2s sported five-rung roof

3-15

Replace any damaged rivets with trimmed NBW castings, using the old rivets to mark locations for the new ones.

ladders at each end. These are easy to model with Precision Scale's brass ladder stock. Cut away three rungs above the fifth rung, and remove all traces of the rungs, **3-18**, with a needle file.

The tops of the stiles are curved, with each at a different height. Bend each stile around a the shank of a screwdriver (or other similar rod) to shape it, **3-19**.

Place the ladder against the model to determine the location of the mounting holes atop the shell. Mark the locations, drill the holes, and test-fit the ladder. Once you're satisfied with the fit, trim the top stiles so they just extend into the shell and glue them in place with CA, **3-20**. I didn't glue them at the bottom, instead letting them rest in holes drilled on the walkway.

Class lights

I used Cal-Scale brass marker lights to represent the distinctive GN classification lights. Start by filing the bottom of the casting flat, then drill a No. 70 hole upward into the casting, **3-21**, taking care to keep the hole straight.

Cut the original mounting post from the marker with a razor saw, then re-shape to the casting with needle

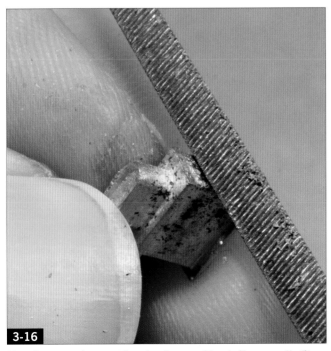

3-16

Many brass castings require cleaning up with a knife or needle file.

3-17

A new exhaust stack was part of an early version change for the RS-2 Glue the new stack in place crosswise to the hood using CA.

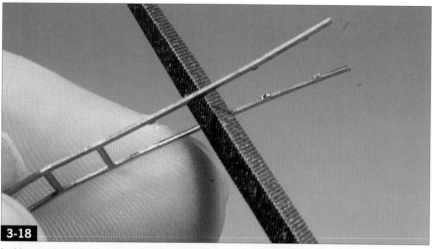

3-18

Ladder stock makes it easy to fashion the RS-2 roof access ladders. Cut away three rungs, then file the insides of the stiles smooth with a needle file.

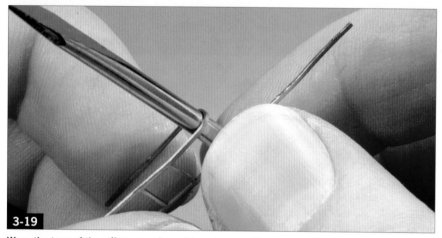

3-19

Wrap the tops of the stiles around a rod to get a smooth curve.

files. Glue a length of .028" wire into the hole as a mounting post, **3-22**. Repeat for the other light, then drill a mounting hole just behind each number board on the long hood end and glue the detail in place with CA.

The Cal-Scale castings have three openings for lenses, but only two are needed for the class lights (forward and side). Fill the remaining opening with a drop of CA, then paint the castings.

These lights could be moved from end to end, so most prototype photos show them on one (usually the long-hood) end. Glue a piece of wire behind the opposite-end number boards to represent the mounting posts.

Grab irons

The last major project on the RS-2 is making the end grab irons. The model includes locating dimples for mounting holes, but not the grabs themselves. Grab irons usually aren't difficult to make, but these are a bit tricky because they follow the curve of the end of the hood.

Drill the mounting holes with a No. 80 bit. Angle the holes on the corners inward slightly. Bend a 90-degree angle in one end of a length of .012" wire. Bend it slightly around a dowel or other rod that's close to the radius of

3-20

The ladder is glued in mounting holes atop the roof, while the bottoms of the stiles rest in holes drilled in the walkway.

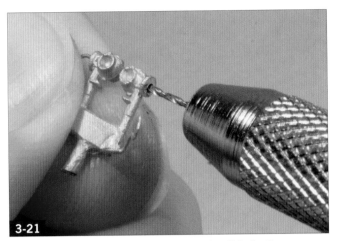

3-21

Drill a mounting hole in the base of the marker light for the new mounting peg.

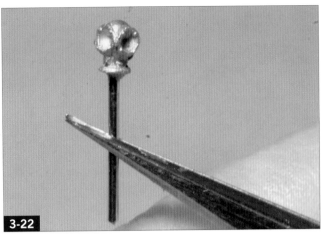

3-22

The .029" wire serves as a mounting post for the class-light casting.

the hood corner, then slip it into the mounting hole and check the fit, **3-23**. Once the shape is correct, bend the other end to fit in its mounting hole, trim the piece, and glue it in place with CA.

GP40-2 pilots

The Rio Grande (and many other Western and Northern railroads) ran their hood-unit diesels with plows on the pilots. Details West and others offer a variety of plows to match various prototypes. Photographs or modeling articles will help you determine the proper plow for your model.

3-23

Pre-bend the curve in the grab iron, then apply it in the mounting hole before bending the final angle on the corner end.

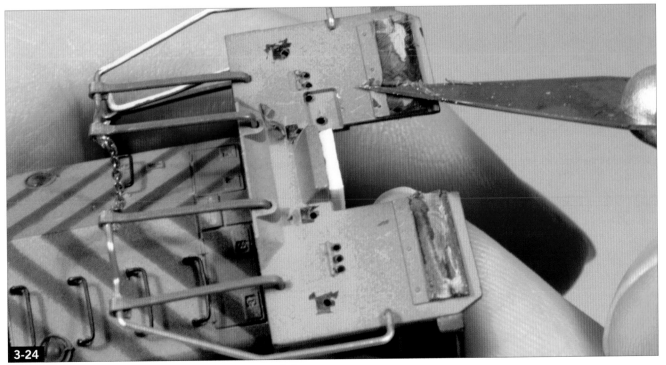

3-24

Shave off all details from the pilots at both ends of the GP40-2.

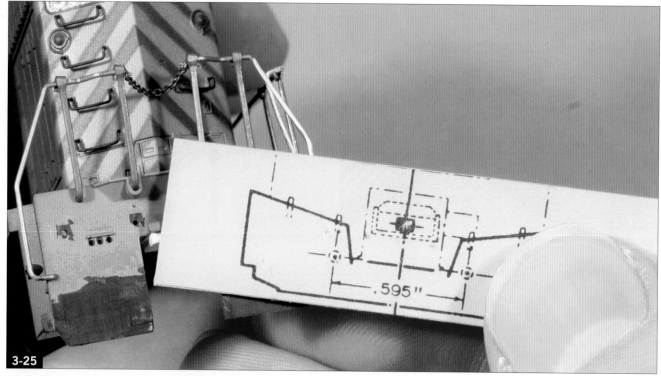

3-25

Details West provides a mounting hole drill template with its plows.

3-26

Cut the pilot plate from .010" styrene and glue it in place across the pilot. Add nut-bolt-washer castings as shown.

3-27

Thread the brackets onto the uncoupling lever, then press the brackets into their mounting holes and secure them with CA.

Both pilots on the Athearn model need to be modified, so start by shaving off all protruding details, 3-24, and sanding the pilots smooth.

Most manufacturers supply a drill-guide template as with the Details West plow, 3-25.

Place the template over the front pilot as instructed, then use a pin to mark mounting-hole locations. Drill the mounting holes and test-fit the plow, making sure it fits squarely on the pilot. Paint it and use CA to glue it in place.

The rear pilot on Rio Grande GP40-2s had a flat plate across the bottom, 3-26. Cut the plate from .010" styrene to fit, cutting angles on the corners to match the pilot. Leave enough room in the center opening for the coupler box to slide into place (see chapter 6 for more on coupler mounting). Glue the plate in place with plastic cement. Add nut-bolt-washer detail

to the pilot plate, then paint the plate to match the pilot.

Both pilots need an uncoupling lever. The Athearn model had molded bumps at the bracket locations. Shave these off and drill mounting holes using these marks as a guide.

Some models will have locating dimples, or the holes for the factory-supplied lever can be used; for others, you're on your own. Make sure the holes align across the pilot.

Headlights

Prototype locomotives use many styles and combinations of headlight housings. You can use prototype photos and modeling articles as a guide.

The simplest headlight conversion is removing a molded-on detail and replacing it with a casting. Remove molded-on headlight details with a knife or detail chisel (upper left), then file or sand the area smooth (upper right). Be careful not to ding or scratch surrounding paint or details. Glue the new headlight casting in place, making sure it's centered and aligned properly. This Burlington Route Atlas GP7 is getting a new upper Mars headlight casting from Custom Finishing and a new lower headlight from Detail Associates (lower left).

Paint the castings and touch up any surrounding paint as on the Proto 2000 SD9 (lower right).

Thread the brackets onto the wire lever, making sure all are oriented properly. Fit them into the mounting holes starting at one end, **3-27**, and hold each in place with a drop of CA. Go down the line until all four brackets are in place.

Cab and nose

Older Athearn models such as this one have a single piece of glazing that fits inside the cab behind the window openings. American Model Builders offers laser-cut window sets that

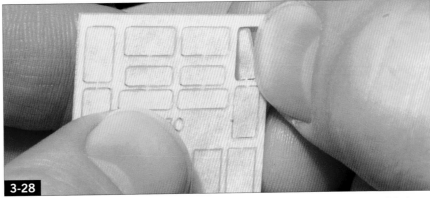

3-28

American Model Builders offers several laser-cut window kits. The pieces pop out of their sheets and press-fit into window openings.

3-29

Paint the frames of the cab's side sliding windows silver.

3-30

Press the laser-cut window into the proper frame, making sure the front surface is flush with the opening.

greatly improve the windows' appearance, **3-28**.

Remove and discard the stock glazing. Paint the inner frames on the side openings silver, **3-29,** with a fine brush. These moldings represent the frames for the sliding windows that can be opened on real locomotives.

The laser-cut windows come with protective backing paper on both surfaces. Pop each window section out as needed, then press it into the appropriate window opening, **3-30**. Once the windows are in place, remove the backing paper from the inside surface.

Make sure each window is flush and level in its opening. To secure the glazing, dip a fine brush in liquid plastic cement. From the inside of the shell, lightly touch the tip of the brush to the joint between the glazing and shell. Don't let the brush touch the surface of the "window" – just the joint. Capillary action will pull the solvent into the joint and hold the glazing. Leave the front protective paper on until after the model has been weathered.

Just as the Burlington GP35 in chapter 2, the Athearn nose requires a headlight. However, as the photos

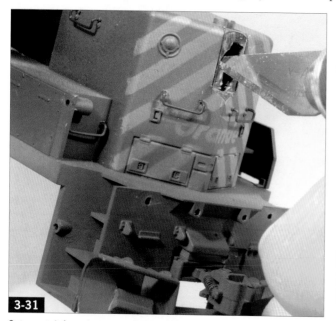

3-31

Cut a notch into the nose slightly wider than the headlight casting.

3-32

Glue the .060" styrene piece into place, then add the headlight casting.

The metal Athearn chassis has a molding line and other imperfections across the fuel tank, and the filler and sight glass details are crude.

show, the mounting is slightly different. Start by cutting a notch into the nose slightly wider than the headlight casting, **3-31**. Cut a piece of .060" styrene sheet to fit the opening, **3-32**.

The styrene piece should be a snug fit side to side, and should stand about .010" above the top surface of the nose. Glue the styrene piece in place with liquid styrene cement. Clean up the headlight casting as necessary and glue it to the styrene with CA.

Underframe and underbody
The underframe and fuel tank on many older models present opportunities for improved appearance. The Athearn chassis and fuel tank are a single metal casting, **3-33**. This casting has some unrealistic ridges, with a couple of crude bumps to represent the fuel filler and sight glass.

Start by removing the motor, trucks, and other hardware from the frame. Smooth the fuel tank, **3-34**, with a large flat file. Use a hacksaw to cut off the filler and sight glass bumps, and smooth that area with a file, **3-35**.

Fuel tank accessories include a dial-type fuel gauge in the tank, a sight glass at the top edge of the tank, and a filler pipe and cap. Check prototype

photos – gauge location and use varied among railroads and locomotives.

Add a Detail Associates fuel gauge by drilling a hole in the side of the fuel tank. A drill press, **3-36**, is the best tool for this, clamping and bracing the

model so the drill bit is perpendicular to the tank.

Start with a small pilot hole (about No. 61) before drilling the final No. 34 hole for the gauge. Glue the gauge in place with CA. Determine the location

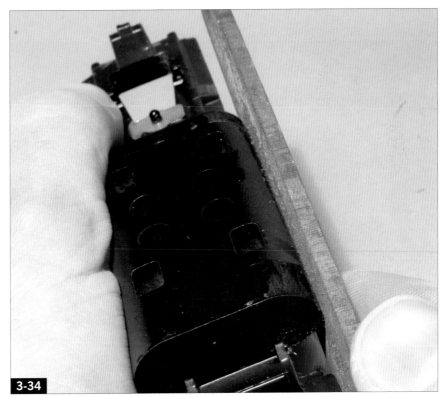

Use a file to smooth the sides of the fuel tank.

3-35

Cut off the filler and sight glass bumps on each side with a hacksaw and smooth the areas with a file.

of the filler pipe and sight glass, making sure these details will clear the bell and air filter details soon to be added to the shell. Drill a hole in the tank for the pipe, then glue it and the sight glass in place, **3-37**. Use a brush or airbrush to paint all visible areas of the tank and chassis black or grimy black.

The air reservoirs, piping, and air filters are quite visible on many prototype locomotives of this era and later. The Athearn model has half of a res-

ervoir molded to the underside of the walkway on the shell. Remove it with a razor saw, **3-38**.

Test-fit the new DA reservoirs on each side. These have molded piping detail on both ends, which I left in place, since it will disappear under the walkway lip.

Cut the molded pipe off the forward end of each reservoir and drill the centers to accept a length of .016" wire. Make mounting pads from .020" x .030" styrene strip and glue the new reservoir in place, **3-39**.

Drill clearance holes through the air filters, **3-40**, for the wire piping. Determine the location of the air filters and remaining piping following prototype photos and the templates and drawings included with the detail parts. Test-fit the shell to the chassis to make sure the filters, reservoir, and fuel tank details all clear each other.

Glue the air filters in place, then add the .015" wire piping, **3-39, 41**. Glue the bell under the walkway on the fireman's side. Once all the details are in place, paint everything grimy black.

Athearn handrails

Athearn models of this era had metal railings and stanchions that required assembly. Although not as

3-36

Use a drill press to drill a mounting hole for the fuel-tank gauge.

Add the fuel filler, sight glass, and gauge on each side of the tank.

finely detailed as today's acetal plastic handrails or after-market cast stanchions and wire handrails, they are extremely durable – an important factor if your model will be transported frequently.

Thread the stanchions onto the handrails, then press the stanchions and handrail ends into place. Add a drop of CA to the handrail where each stanchion will meet it, **3-42**, then slide the stanchion into place, make sure it's vertical, and crimp it to the handrail using needle-nose pliers.

Rio Grande locomotives had drop steps, so an opening needs to be made between the innermost stanchions at each end. Trim the end handrail, then crimp the stanchions in place. Press short lengths of .012" wire into the notch at the top of each middle stanchion, **3-43**, then glue a length of A-Line chain in place, looping the end link over the wire.

Paint the handrails with a brush. I coated my handrails in grimy black to match the weathered appearance of the locomotive. Then a little white paint helps set off the rails at the corner steps.

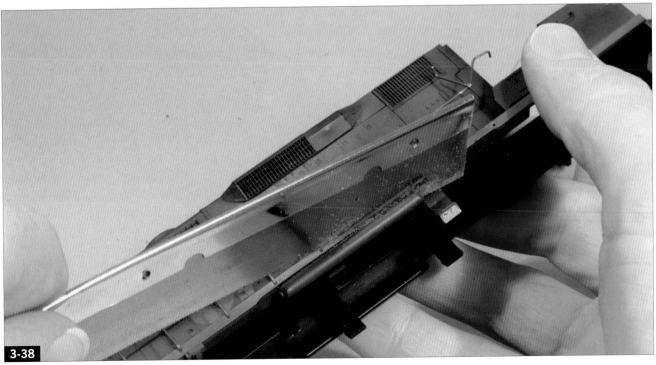

3-38

Cut off the molded reservoir from the shell with a razor saw.

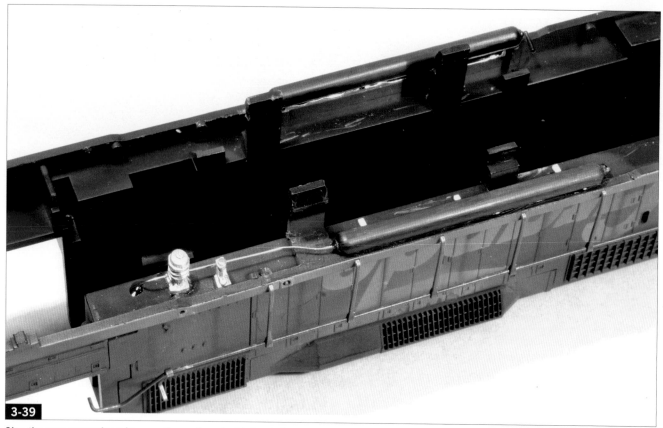

3-39

Glue the new reservoir on its mounting pads and add the air filters. The wire passes behind the small dryer and through the large filter, then is glued to the shell.

3-40

Drill No. 77 holes through each air filter so the wire piping can pass through them.

3-41

Finish the piping on both sides and add the bell on a styrene mounting pad.

Miscellaneous details

Add a drop step and m.u. stand to the end platforms of the GP40-2, **3-44**.

The remaining details including lift rings, horns, cab sunshades, windshield wipers, m.u. and train line hoses, and headlight lenses are like those in chapter 1. See chapter 6 for details on coupler choice and mounting.

The Athearn model included truck sideframes that matched the most common style found on real GP40-2s, with a damping strut on one axle, a single brake cylinder, and two inboard brake shoes, **3-45**. However, the Rio Grande's GP40-2s ran the older style of EMD truck, with two cylinders, no strut, and four brake shoes. Correcting

this was simply a matter of pulling off the sideframes and replacing them with the proper ones. I also added a brake line between the two cylinders. Number board decals were added to each model following examples in chapter 5.

After all these modifications, your model will need a little paint touch up. The GN required quite a bit of both

3-42

New handrail details are much more realistic than the stock versions. Here the author places a drop of CA on a handrail, then slides the stanchion into place and crimps it with pliers.

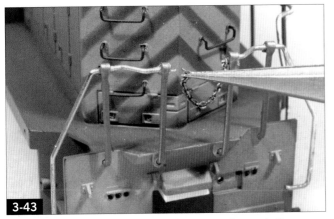

3-43

Add a length of chain between the middle stanchions to indicate access to the next locomotive is closed. Ends are hooked over bits of .012" wire glued in the stanchions.

3-44

Glue the drop step and m.u. stand in place on each platform.

orange (Polly Scale No. 414224 GN Orange) around the number boards and green (Modelflex No. 1616 Brunswick Green) over the old stack area. The Rio Grande model used black, grimy black, and orange (Polly Scale No. 414254 D&RGW Orange).

The models are now ready for weathering, as described in chapter 5. If you're game for even more-extensive body modifications, turn the page and we'll create a truly distinctive model with some heavy cutting into a diesel shell.

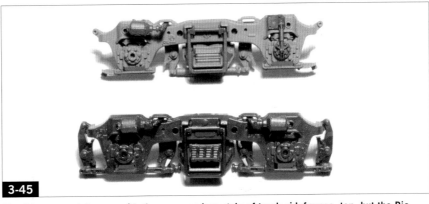

3-45

The Athearn model came with the more modern style of truck sideframes, top, but the Rio Grande's GP40-2s used the older style, bottom.

CHAPTER FOUR

Major surgery

Some major body alterations turned a Proto 2000 GP9 into a model of a Paducah rebuild GP10, based on real locomotives rebuilt by the Illinois Central in the 1960s and '70s.

Sometimes the only way to get the locomotive you want is by making extensive body modifications or by combining two models to make one (called kitbashing). The need for such conversions comes up frequently when modeling real locomotives that have been rebuilt or modified. Although chopping shells means you'll have to paint and decal them, the effort results in a model that you can't buy off the shelf. In this chapter we'll take a kitbashing project from start to finish, then look at some individual alterations that can be made to decorated models.

4-1

Five years after being rebuilt, GP10 No. 8078 displays quite a bit of weathering as it leads a train through Rock Rapids, Iowa, in 1975.

Rebuilding Paducah Rebuilds

I'd been meaning to build a model of Illinois Central No. 8078 for years, as it was the first prototype locomotive I ever photographed: Rock Rapids, Iowa, summer 1975, Kodak Hawkeye camera, loaded with 127 color film.

Number 8078 was one of hundreds of diesels the IC's Paducah, Ky., shops rebuilt from EMD GP7 and GP9 locomotives during the late 1960s and early 1970s. The work involved rebuilding the engine and other internal components, as well as chopping the nose.

These diesels became known as "Paducah Rebuilds," and the railroad designated them as GP8s (rebuilt from GP7s) and GP10s (rebuilt from GP9s). The locomotives shared a common look, but headlight location (upper only or upper and nose) and style; exhaust stack spacing; air filter style; louver placement; and fan style and placement varied among individual engines. As with any modeling project, the best way to achieve accuracy was to pick a specific locomotive at a specific time.

I had my original 1975 photo, **4-1**, and I was lucky enough to locate two

4-2

Illinois Central GP10 No. 8078 was just two months out of the shop when this photo was taken in June 1970. Note the lack of snow hoods on the air filter atop the hood. *John Ingles; J. David Ingles collection*

4-3

This view shows No. 8078 during rebuilding in April 1970, before passing through the paint shop. The notched access door on the side of the nose is standing open. *John Ingles; J. David Ingles collection*

additional images: a 1970 action photo showing No. 8078 freshly in service, **4-2**, and a lucky shot, an under-construction view of the opposite side, **4-3**.

This diesel shows how appearance changed: Between 1970 and 1975, the number boards were changed (from white numbers on a black background to a different style of black-on-white numbers), snow shields were added to the roof-mounted Horst air filter, and the rerail frog was removed. And, the locomotive showed weathering worthy of its five years of service.

With any such project, determine the model that will best match the real thing. In this case, a Proto 2000 model of a Phase II GP9 was the best choice, **4-4**, with hood louvers and roof-top fans that matched the prototype locomotive. An undecorated model

4-4

This project used the shell of a Proto 2000 Phase II GP9 and the chassis of a Proto 2000 GP20.

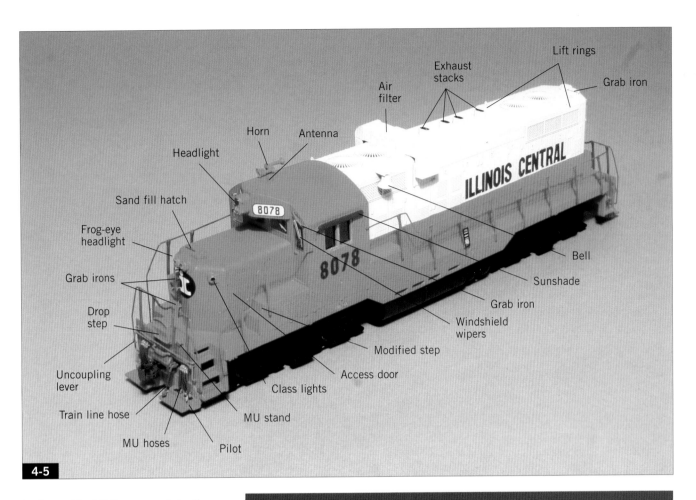

Exhaust stacks • Lift rings • Air filter • Grab iron • Horn • Antenna • Headlight • ILLINOIS CENTRAL • Sand fill hatch • 8078 • 8078 • Frog-eye headlight • Bell • Grab irons • Sunshade • Drop step • Grab iron • Windshield wipers • Uncoupling lever • Modified step • Class lights • Access door • Train line hose • MU stand • MU hoses • Pilot

4-5

is always ideal. Mine was originally painted for the Rock Island – hence the maroon handrails and fans – but the original owner had stripped the paint. If your only option is a decorated model, you can often remove paint by soaking the shell in 90 percent rubbing alcohol or a commercial paint remover, such as Chameleon or ELO. Be sure to test paint removers before submerging the whole model.

Don't be discouraged if you initially can't locate a needed out-of-production model. If it's been made, it's for sale out there somewhere. The Internet has been a boon for finding out-of-production models – look through eBay listings as well as the online listings of hobby dealers.

Nose

Let's start with the most challenging task, chopping the nose, **4-5**, so the rest of the project will seem less daunting. Disassemble the engine and remove all details from the top and sides of the nose, including the sand filler hatch, grab irons, and classification lights.

Illinois Central Paducah Rebuild Parts List

A-Line
29200 windshield wipers

Cannon & Co.
1004 door

Custom Finishing
109 bell
260 Horst air filter

Des Plaines Hobbies
2005 cab front

Detail Associates
1002 headlight, Pyle Gyralite (upper)
1004 headlight, Pyle dual (nose)
1017 classification lights
1401 drop steps
1501 m.u. stands
1801 antenna, can type
2202 grab irons
2204 uncoupling levers
2208 pilots

2402 exhaust stacks (2 packs)
2809 brake cylinder air line
3002 sand fill hatches

Details West
175 horn, Nathan P3
265 m.u. hose cluster set

Kadee
58 couplers

MV Products
23 headlight lenses

Microscale
87-27 Illinois Central decals

Miniatronics
12-310-05 Yeloglo LED

ShellScale
103 number board decals

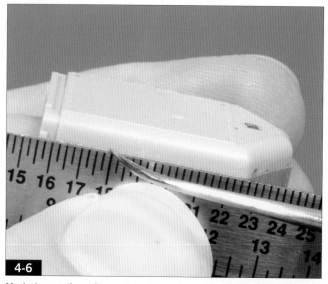

4-6

Mark the cut line with masking tape, then use a straightedge to guide the scriber around the nose.

4-7

Cut off the top of the nose with a razor saw, following the scored line.

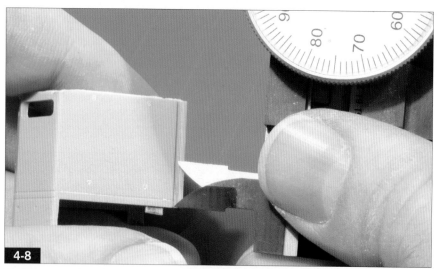

4-8

Mark the second cut line on the nose, then score and cut it as with the first.

4-9

Glue the two nose pieces together. If you measure correctly the first time, a styrene spacer won't be needed!

Mark a line around the top of the nose for the first cut, **4-6**. The exact location isn't critical – the important thing is that the cut be level around the nose and above the number boards, as we'll need them later. Use masking tape to mark the line, and when you're sure it's level, use a scriber to score the shell. Remove the tape and score the line with a hobby knife deep enough to provide a starting groove for a razor saw, **4-7**. Cut through the shell until the top of the nose is free.

Mark a second cut line up from the bottom of the nose, **4-8**, so that the height of the combined sections is a scale 39". Allow a bit of extra material to account for the width of the saw blade. I didn't, which is why you see a styrene spacer in the photos.

Once the lower section is cut, clean up the mating surfaces with a hobby knife and fine sandpaper. Make sure the sections mate with a minimum of gaps, and that the top is level, **4-9**. Align the pieces carefully, then apply liquid plastic cement from inside.

After the glue dries, fill any gaps or visible seams with putty or CA. Fill the remaining grab iron holes as well, along with the horizontal grooves at the bottom of the hood. Sand off the door detail from the left side of the nose by rubbing it flat against a piece of sandpaper. Sand all of these areas smooth.

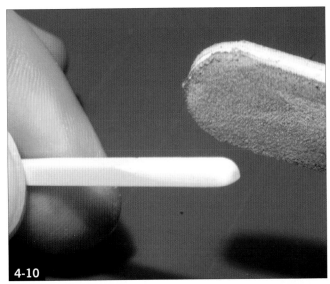

4-10

Use a hobby knife and sanding stick to shape the styrene strip for the frog-eye headlight housing.

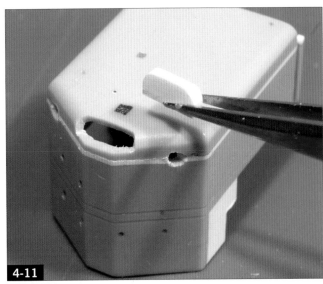

4-11

Cut a notch in the top of the nose for the frog-eye housing, then glue it in place. Note the mounting holes for the new classification lights.

Paducah rebuilds had a variety of headlight configurations. The 8078 ran with what are commonly known as "frog eye" headlights, as the headlight backing is a rounded piece of steel that protrudes from the nose.

Make this piece from a strip of ⅛"-square styrene, **4-10**. Use a hobby knife and sanding stick to carve the strip roughly to shape, comparing it frequently with the Detail Associates casting.

Once the piece has been shaped, cut a notch in the nose for the frog eye, **4-11**. Pause frequently to check the fit against the styrene piece. When you have a tight fit, glue the piece in the notch with styrene cement, making sure the front face is vertical and that it is square across the front of the nose. Once it dries, fill any gaps with CA or putty and sand it to final shape, **4-12**. Glue the DA headlight casting in place with plastic cement.

If you don't want to illuminate the headlight, you can simply glue MV lenses in place after the model is painted. To light the headlight, start by drilling straight into the casting to provide a hole for the lens. Drill into the styrene frog-eye housing, but be careful not to drill out the back of it.

Next, drill holes at an angle into the frog eye from inside the shell, **4-13**, to meet the holes drilled through the headlight casting. I turned my own clear plastic lenses as explained

4-12

Fill any gaps around the headlight housing with CA and sand it to shape. The sand hatch, class lights, and door have also been added.

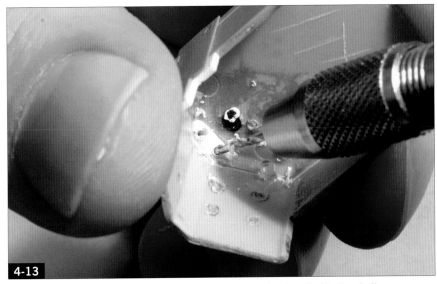

4-13

To illuminate the nose headlight, drill holes into the casting from inside the shell.

4-14

Paint the inside of the nose black, then add epoxy behind the lenses.

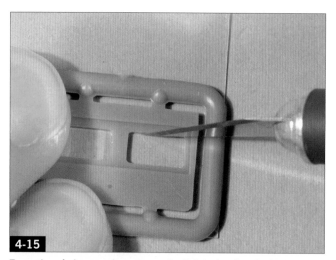

4-15

Trace the window on clear styrene by lightly drawing the blade backward around the edge of the opening.

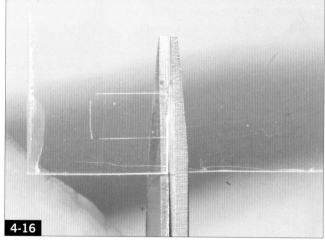

4-16

Use fine scissors to cut the windows out of the clear styrene sheet.

in chapter 2 to fit snugly in the holes drilled in the casting. Paint the inside of the nose shell black to keep light from showing through the plastic.

Glue the lenses in place with liquid plastic cement. Fill the holes from behind with five-minute epoxy, **4-14**. This will help direct the light from the chassis-mounted LED (more on

that in a bit) to the headlight lenses. Cover the lenses with liquid masking or small circles of masking tape before painting the model.

Drill grab iron holes in the nose, using the old filled holes as a guide for the new wire drop-style grabs. Install the new classification lights, **4-12** in new mounting holes. These castings

are molded in clear styrene – glue them in place and mask them as with the headlights.

Mount the new sand filler hatch to the nose, along with the lower grab iron and the nose-top iron. Leave off the top two grabs on the front until after the model is painted and the nose herald decal is added.

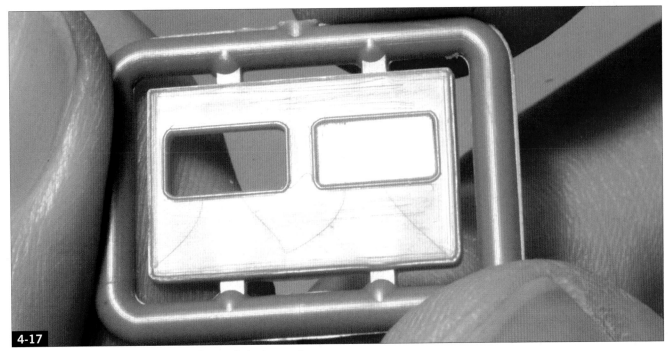

4-17

Test-fit the clear styrene glazing until it fits snugly in the opening.

Cab and steps

Des Plaines Hobbies offers a plastic casting with window openings that fills the gap in the front of the cab. Before gluing the piece in place, decide how you want to treat the windshields. The casting includes a gap in the rear to allow adding a piece of clear styrene. This will work fine. However, even though the detail piece is fairly thin, the glazing will appear slightly recessed.

For a more realistic flush fit, cut clear styrene for the openings. Start by placing the casting face down atop a piece of .015" clear styrene. Lightly trace the opening using a hobby knife, **4-15**. By pulling the blade backward as shown, the knife won't cut the casting.

Use small, sharp scissors to cut the glazing along the marked lines, **4-16**. (The common scribe-and-snap technique doesn't work well for clear styrene, as the edges will crystallize.) A flat needle file works well for rounding the corners. Test-fit the glazing until it fits the opening, **4-17**. Set the window pieces aside — we'll add them after the model is painted.

It may take a couple of tries to get pieces that fit properly. For this project, I cut the first one correctly on the first try, but it took three attempts to get

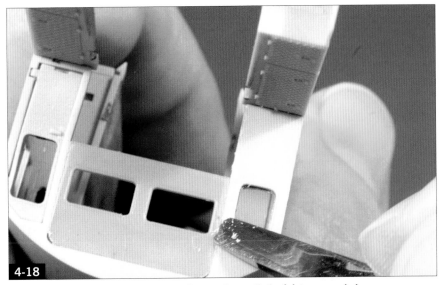

4-18

Glue the window piece in place, then clean and smooth the joints as needed.

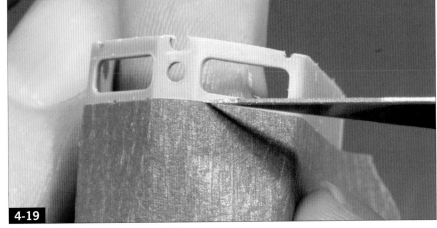

4-19

Trim the number boards from the GP9 nose. Be sure the cut is level.

4-20

Glue the clear number board casting in place, then cut it straight across the back.

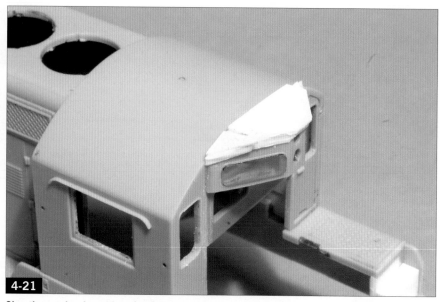

4-21

Glue the number board housing in place, then glue styrene filler atop it above the curve of the cab roof.

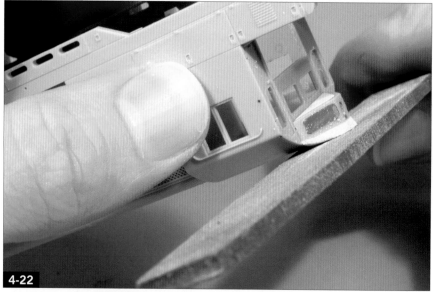

4-22

File the styrene atop the number board area until it matches the cab roof.

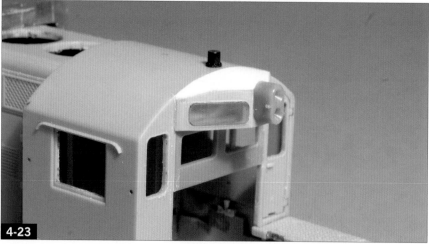

4-23

The completed number board housing blends with the roof.

the second piece. Take your time and don't be discouraged if the first piece or two don't work.

Glue the cab-front casting in place with liquid cement, making sure it's aligned precisely with the shell's cab front. Once it dries, sand and smooth the joints as needed, 4-18. Be careful not to damage the window gasket detail on the casting or door. Drill mounting holes for the windshield wipers at this time.

You can add the new number board housing two ways: by cutting the housing from a Proto 2000 GP20 shell, or the method I chose, cutting the GP9s number boards from the nose and adding styrene filler.

Trim the number board section from the front of the nose, 4-19. Glue the clear headlight/number board casting in place behind it to make it strong and solid, then use a razor saw to trim this piece straight across, 4-20, so it fits squarely to the front of the cab.

Glue this piece in place with liquid plastic cement, making sure that it's level and that the bottom of the number board housing is .040" above the top of the windshield. Glue several pieces of sheet styrene above the casting so it's just above the height of the cab roof, 4-21.

Once this dries, shape the styrene filler with a file or sanding block to match the curve of the cab roof, 4-22.

4-24

Cut the forward box from the walkway with a razor saw.

Fill any gaps with putty or CA, then keep repeating the process until the area is smooth, **4-23**.

The forward box on the walkway on the left side needs to be removed. Trim away the step guard from in front of the box and set it aside. Cut off the box, **4-24**, with a razor saw, then clean up the area with a knife. Patch this area with .040" sheet styrene cut to fit, **4-25**. The step guard on the right side also needs to be removed.

Test-fit the nose to the walkway/cab. Add a piece of .040" sheet styrene to fill the gap on the left side and notch it to fit the new step area. The nose has an access door on the left side. Trim the tabs from the rear of the Cannon & Co. door, then use a sanding block on the back of the door to thin it. The door must also be notched to clear the step, **4-26**, just as on the real thing. Glue the door in place with liquid cement.

Body

One set of louvers must be removed on each side, **4-27**, on the first tall door behind the cab, just below the

4-25

Rebuild the step area using .040" styrene. Add .040" styrene to the gap in the nose, cutting it to match the new step area

new air filter. Carefully shave off the louvers with a Micro-Mark chisel, then smooth the area with sandpaper.

This hood door must also be shortened to make room for a plate under the air filter. Use the plate as a template to mark the cut line on the door, then with a chisel, trim the top of the

door to the line, **4-28**. Glue the plate in place with CA.

Trim all details off of the pilot, smooth the area with a file, and glue the new pilot details in place with liquid cement, **4-29**.

Fill the holes for the original drop step and drill out the holes for the

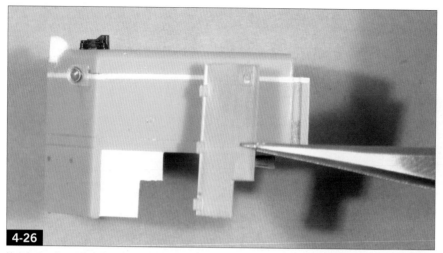

4-26

Notch the Cannon & Co. door to fit above the steps on the side of the nose.

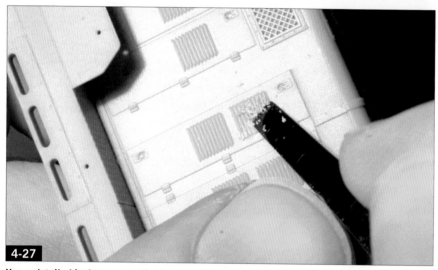

4-27

Use a detail chisel to remove the top set of louvers from the first tall door behind the cab.

uncoupling lever to match the Detail Associates brackets. Add the uncoupling lever, drop step, and m.u. stand, which must be cut down to a single socket from the original two-socket housing.

Paducah rebuilds have four exhaust stacks instead of two as on a standard Geep. Cut off the original stacks with a knife and chisel and sand the areas smooth.

The stacks of some rebuilds were evenly spaced, but on others, such as 8078, the two center stacks were closer together. Place them so that, from the front of the rear roof panel, the stack centers measure a scale 30", 5'-6", 7'-0", and 9'-9". Glue the new stacks in place with liquid cement, **4-30**, keeping them centered side-to-side, and following the proper spacing.

Add the remaining details, including the can-type antenna and horn atop the cab roof, **4-29**, the headlight on the front of the number-board housing, and the sand hatches. Drill holes for grab irons on the end of the long hood and the roof.

The large yoke-style air-filter housing atop the long hood was a prominent spotting feature of Paducah rebuilds. Number 8078 ran with a Horst filter, which was – as the prototype photo in **4-2** shows – originally

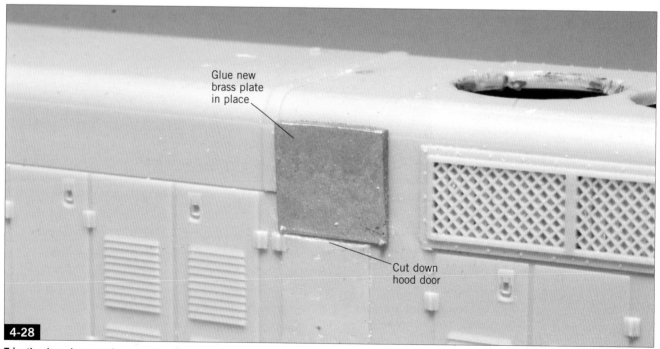

Glue new brass plate in place

Cut down hood door

4-28

Trim the door down so the new plate fits above it.

installed without snow shields. Many of these diesels eventually received the shields, **4-1**.

Detail Associates and Custom Finishing both offer this detail, but the DA part is designed for the old Athearn GP7, which has a wider-than-prototype hood. The brass CF part fits the scale-width Proto 2000 hood, but the casting requires some cleaning up. Remove any burrs, ridges, or other imperfections from the casting with needle files before gluing it in place with CA, **4-31**.

The shell is now ready for painting as described in chapter 5.

Final details

Some details have to wait until after painting. Install the remaining grab irons, then paint them appropriately. Paint the rooftop fan blades grimy black, snap them in place in the grills, and add the fan housings to the roof. Use a drop of CA under each to hold it in place.

Add the windshields and other clear glazing to the cab, then glue the windshield wipers in place. Remove the masking from the nose lenses and add any remaining lenses. The upper headlight housing needs a red MV lens in the top and a clear one in the bottom.

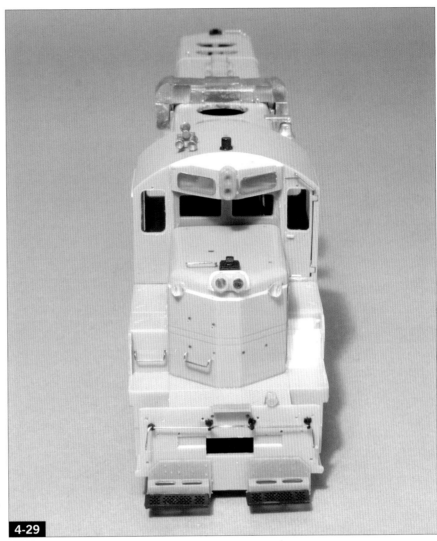

4-29 Add the pilots, footboards, uncoupling lever, drop step base, and m.u. stand.

4-30 Glue the new exhaust stacks in place, keeping them properly spaced and centered side to side.

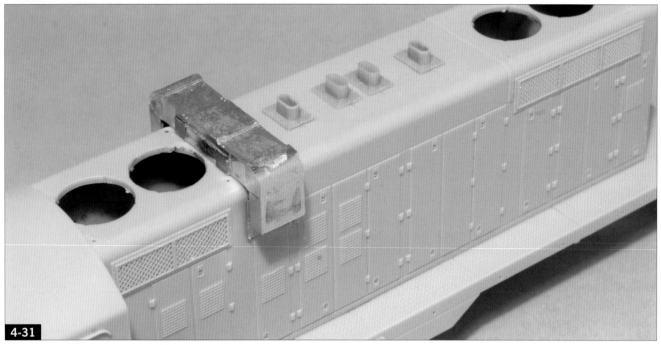

4-31

Once the stacks are in place, add the Horst air filter.

4-32

Make the sunshade by gluing painted aluminum foil to a wire bracket.

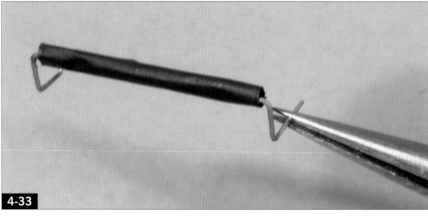

4-33

Wrap the aluminum foil around the bracket to simulate the canvas of the real thing.

The Paducah Rebuilds were equipped with canvas cab sunshades mounted on a bracket that could be extended from the cab. I modeled them in the collapsed position.

Start by making a scale 5'-0"-long bracket from .019" wire and paint the ends of the bracket orange. Paint a scale 4'-6"-wide piece of aluminum foil grimy black. Glue one end of it to the bracket with CA, **4-32**, then wrap it twice around the wire and trim it so the end will be hidden when it's installed, **4-33**. Glue the end of the foil in place with a touch of CA. You'll need mounting holes on the cab side to match the bracket so that the shade rests above the window; glue the shade in place.

Paint the Details West m.u. hose group castings and glue them in place. Add the Cal-Scale train line hose.

Although the cab doesn't have interior detail, I added a seated Preiser figure as an engineer, gluing him to a piece of styrene strip glued to the inside of the cab, **4-34**.

Chassis and trucks

You can modify the GP9 chassis to work with the rebuilt model, but I substituted a GP20 chassis that I had from an earlier project, 4. The main advan-

4-34

Add some life to the cab by gluing a seated figure to a piece of styrene and gluing it to the inside cab wall.

tage to this is that the front weight is ready for the low nose. If you choose the original chassis, use a hacksaw to cut the nose weight to match the height of the low nose. Be sure to allow a scale foot or so of clearance.

To illuminate the nose headlight, I chose a Yeloglo LED from Miniatronics. These are very bright and don't get hot like bulbs, so they can be used without the risk of melting plastic. To provide room, I reshaped the nose weight with a file, **4-35**. Provide enough room for the wires as well as the LED.

This Proto model already had LEDs, so adding the new one was a matter of cutting the old one off, then soldering the new LED and its resistor to the cut-off leads. Cover all bare wires with electrical tape.

I added a DCC decoder while I was at it, which was a simple matter of removing the model's circuit board and plugging an eight-pin decoder in place (I used one from NCE, but many other plug-in decoders would work as well).

If you use a GP20 chassis, remove the plastic fuel and air tank casting from the GP9 model and swap it to the GP20 chassis.

I spruced up the truck sideframes a bit by adding a speed recorder cable to the rear axle of the lead truck on the right side. This required drilling a ¹⁄₁₆" hole in the center of the journal on the

sideframe, **4-36**, and pressing the detail part in place. The "cable" supplied by DA is a length of wire with plastic insulation. Pull the wire out, then slip the insulation over the cable anchor,

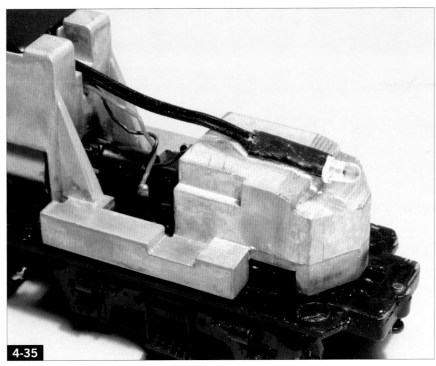

4-35

Cut a gap in the nose for the LED with a file. Wrap the wires and LED leads in electrical tape, then glue it in place.

4-36

The speed recorder required a hole in the center of the journal on the truck sideframe.

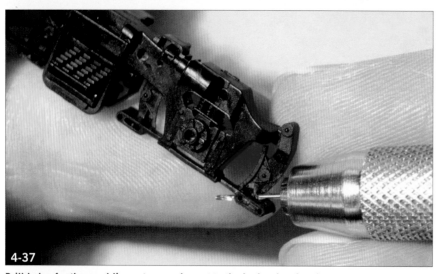

4-37

Drill holes for the sand lines at an angle next to the brake shoe bracket.

4-38

Slide the sand line wire through the holes, shape the wire, and glue in place with CA.

which in turn snaps in place in the center hole of the new journal. I had to enlarge the opening in the insulation slightly by slowly turning a No. 80 drill bit into the end. Add a bit of CA to the anchor and slip the insulation into place.

I also added air lines between the brake cylinders on the truck chassis, as well as sand lines, **4-37**. To do this, drill a No. 74 hole at a sharp angle next to the brake shoe bracket. Drill another hole at the top of the bracket, then slip a piece of .022" wire in place, **4-38**. When the shape looks correct, add a drop of CA to each hole. Paint the wires black.

After the sideframe is added to the chassis, bend the tops of the sand lines so they are just short of touching the chassis, **4-39**. Drill a hole in the frame and slip the speed-recorder cable into it, but don't glue it.

Assembly

You can now screw the shell into place on the chassis and add the couplers.

Install the handrails. The original left-front handrails will no longer fit because of the step modifications, so I substituted a left-front handrail from a Proto 2000 GP20.

Brush-paint the handrails orange. It took two coats to cover the maroon railings on my locomotive. Had the original railings been black, I would have started with a primer coat of medium or light gray.

Since acetal plastic doesn't take paint well, once the handrails are painted, avoid handling them. If some paint gets chipped or rubs off, touch up the area as soon as possible.

Add an ACI label to a stanchion on each side. Cut a piece of .010" styrene to match the label from the Microscale set, paint the plastic orange, glue it to the appropriate stanchion, and add the decal.

The model is now complete. You can decide if you want to keep it in this pristine condition, or – as I did – weather it to make it look as though it's been in service for awhile. See chapter 5 for tips on weathering.

4-39

Drill a hole in the frame for the speed-recorder cable, and paint all wires and cables black.

Special effects on CB&Q E units

Many of the Chicago, Burlington & Quincy's silver E units had distinctive stainless-steel side panels, **4-40, 41**. This gave them a unique look, as the panels have a different sheen compared to the painted areas of the locomotives.

Proto 2000 has offered its E7 and E8 models in this paint scheme, **4-42**, but I wanted to upgrade them with simulated stainless panels (and see-through screens on the E7). I also wanted to add details to reflect the appearance of the real locomotives in the mid-1960s period that I model.

4-40

Many of the Burlington Route's E units sported stainless-steel side panels, as on E7 9932B, shown at Denver in 1969. Note the m.u. hatches on either side of the upper headlight. *Hol Wagner; J. David Ingles collection*

4-41

By the 1960s, Burlington E units sported grab irons on the nose, along with grabs above the windows and sides, spark arrestors, and upgraded air horns. Also note the m.u. access hatches on either side of the upper headlight. E8 No. 9937B is shown here in 1966.

Body details

Starting in the 1950s, many railroads modified their cab diesels by adding grab irons up the side of the nose and/or across its top, **4-43**. The exact placement varied by railroad. The Burlington also provided a bottom step with an angled steel strip at the bottom of the body. Use a scale 7'-0" piece of .060" Evergreen styrene L-angle strip

to model this, gluing it in place as in the photos of the finished models.

The hardest part of modeling the nose grabs is locating the drill starting points and making sure that all grabs are in proper alignment. To make it easier to mark the drill locations, place pieces of masking tape on the shell, **4-44**. You can then use a pencil, straightedge, and scale rule to measure

and mark the grab iron spots on the tape. This is a much more forgiving technique than trying to mark the spots directly on the model.

Check your prototype photos or drawings for reference, as placement varied significantly among railroads (and often among locomotives of the same railroad). Use a pin to mark the locations through the tape onto the

4-42

The Proto 2000 E8 comes from the manufacturer in the CB&Q's basic silver-and-red passenger scheme. The model includes many separate details, but still requires a few more – along with stainless side panels – to accurately match its prototype.

4-43

Bare-Metal sides, grab irons, and other details have made this a much more realistic model.

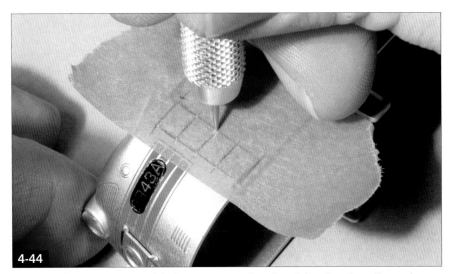

4-44

Place masking tape on the model, then measure and mark grab iron locations. Use a pin or sharp scriber to transfer the marks to the body.

4-45

Use the pin marks as a guide for drilling holes for the grabs and NBW castings.

model, then drill the holes in the shell, **4-45**.

Making a template will speed the process (see photo 14 in chapter 2). Be sure to include a reference mark for locating the template, and tape the template in place to make sure it doesn't move while you're marking the grab locations. Add grabs atop the nose as well, **4-46**.

Burlington E8, E7 parts list

American Model Builders
223 steam generator vents (E7)

Bare-Metal Foil
001 chrome foil

Detail Associates
2201 grab irons with NBW castings
2206 eye bolts
2215 ladder grab irons
2701 grille (E9)
2711 screen (E7)

Details West
118 steam generator (2 sets)

MV Products
300 class light lenses

Microscale
87-98 CB&Q E unit decals
87-527 diesel decals (m.u. hatches)
87-793 diesel decals (builder's plates)

Overland
9563 spark arrestors (E9)

Precision Scale
39133 antenna, firecracker

ShellScale
105 number board decals

Tichy
3021 grab irons, 18"

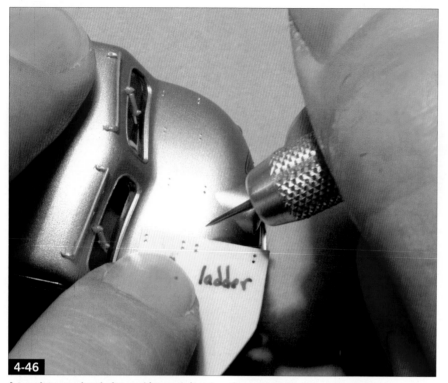

4-46

A template was handy for marking grab iron locations across the top of the nose.

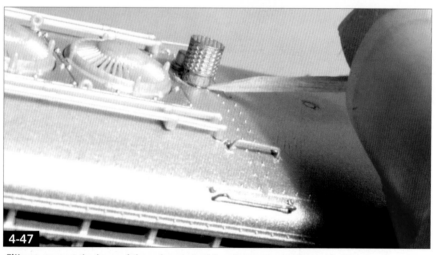

4-47

Fill any gaps at the base of the exhaust stack/spark arrestor casting with CA.

You can add just the grabs themselves, or add nut-bolt-washer castings as I did. This is a bit of extra work, but they look sharp when installed.

Add the rooftop grabs and ladder grabs as the photos show. The use and placement of these varied among prototypes and eras, so check photos whenever possible.

The Burlington's E units had spark arrestors installed over the exhaust stacks. The Overland detail parts are cast into the stacks, so installing them first required removing the model's molded-on stacks. After installing the new casting, add CA around the base with a toothpick, **4-47**, to hide any gaps, then paint the spark arrestor and stack silver.

I couldn't find an exact match for the Burlington's unusual horn arrangement on its 1960's E units, with two forward-facing horns (one small and one large) on the right and a single medium-length trumpet on the left. I modified a three-chime horn casting left over from a Kato locomotive.

Start by trimming the middle-length bell from the casting, then drill a No. 70 hole through the short bell, **4-48**. Trim the short bell flush with the mounting bracket, then move it to the other side of the bracket so it's facing the same direction as the large bell. Press a straight pin through the bracket from the rear, trim off the point, and press the short bell in place on the pin, **4-49**.

The pin will hold the horn securely in place, as glue won't work on the acetal plastic parts. The horn can then

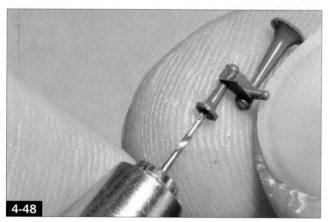

4-48

Drill a hole through the short horn. This will be the mounting hole when the bell is moved to the other side.

4-49

A cut-off pin pressed through the bracket and into the short bell holds it in place.

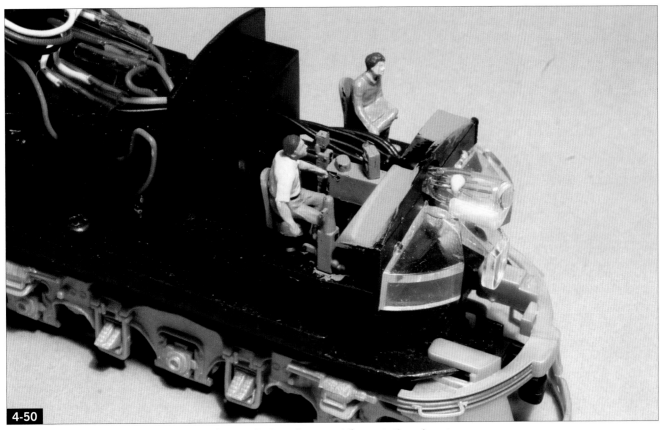

4-50

Paint the cab interior gray and the exposed wires black, then glue seated figures to the cab seats.

be installed on the roof. The left-side horn with the mid-length bell came from my scrap box (a lesson in never throwing away extra detail parts).

Add the antenna and classification light lenses.

The Proto cab has some basic detailing, including control stands, seats, and figures, but everything's molded in black plastic. I gave the interior a basic upgrade by removing the unpainted figures, adding a pair of Preiser seated figures, and giving the interior a coat of light flat gray – except for the wires, which received a coat of flat black, **4-50**.

As with many cab units, the Burlington's E units received m.u. connections. Some railroads left the hoses in place, even when the locomotive was leading (such as the Northern Pacific F unit in chapter 2). Others, like the Burlington, removed the hoses, but the mounting pipes remained in place.

4-51

Make mounting pipes for nose m.u. hoses with short pieces of .029" wire.

4-52

Decals are an excellent way of modeling the m.u. hatches on the nose.

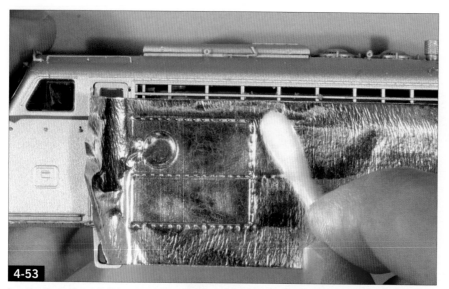

4-53

Lay the Bare-Metal Foil in place, then begin gently pressing it in place with your fingers and a cotton swab.

4-54

Use a toothpick to press the foil into tight areas and around raised details.

Model these by drilling four No. 70 holes just above the anticlimber on the right side and adding small pieces of .029" wire that have been bent at the ends, **4-51**. Glue the wires in place and paint them grimy black. Add another on the left side.

Most EMD Es and Fs had small hatches on either side of the upper headlight to cover the socket for the multiple-unit cable. The best way I've found to model these is using Microscale decal set no. 87-527, which includes black decal outlines for these details, **4-52**.

Stainless sides

Now for the step that will give the model its distinctive appearance. Begin by removing all of the side grab irons, railings, and steps from the shell to provide a smooth surface for the foil.

I used Bare-Metal Foil (chrome) for the stainless side panels. Popular with airplane and auto modelers, Bare-Metal is a thin, flexible, adhesive-backed foil. When working with Bare-Metal Foil, use a brand-new knife blade. A blade that's even a bit dull will tear the foil or leave a ragged edge. Also, make sure the model is clean and free of dust.

Cut a sheet large enough to cover half of one side (the middle door provides a dividing point). Peel the foil from its backing sheet, being careful

4-55

Use the batten strips as a guide for the knife in trimming the foil.

4-56

Trim and remove the foil from the round side windows and sand-fill hatches.

not to wrinkle or tear it. Lay the foil loosely on the side and begin pressing it in place with your finger on one end, **4-53**. Use a cotton swab and your finger to lightly press the foil in place around each panel, continuing from panel to panel while making sure no wrinkles or folds develop. If the foil folds or tears, remove the piece and start over.

Once the piece is in place, burnish the foil to the raised details, such as the batten strip. A good tool for this is a toothpick that's been trimmed to a chisel tip, **4-54**. Work slowly and press the foil tightly along all raised details.

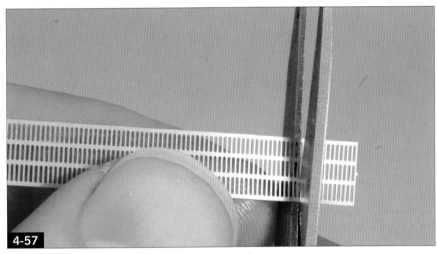

4-57

Trim the new stainless side grille with fine, sharp scissors.

4-58

The E7 received many of the same modifications as the E9, with the addition of see-through screens.

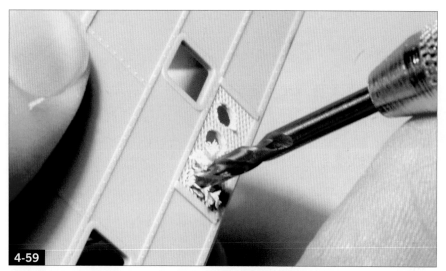

4-59

Drill out the molded screens along the top of each side.

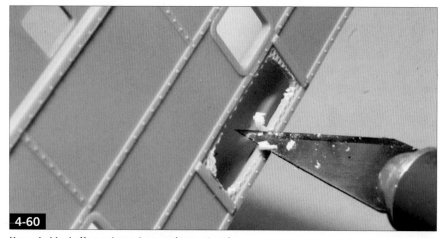

4-60

Use a hobby knife to shave the opening to the trim.

Don't drag the toothpick, or the foil will tear. Instead, press a section, lift the toothpick, move it, and do it again. It takes some time, but the results will be worth it.

Again using a fresh knife blade, carefully trim the foil at the edges along the batten strips, **4-55**, letting the knife tip follow the batten strip as a guide. Trim around details such as the portholes and sand-fill hatches, and remove the foil from those areas, **4-56**.

I wanted my model to represent an E9 instead of an E8, so I removed the model's original stainless-steel grilles with horizontal openings and glued a new vertical-slit Detail Associates grille in place. The new grille required trimming, **4-57**, best done with fine scissors. I used Microscale Kristal Klear to glue it in place, applying it to full length of the horizontal pieces in the grille opening, then laying the new grille in place.

Decals

The "Burlington" side lettering needs to be applied with decals, since the foil covered the factory lettering. Apply the decals as described in chapter 5. It's a bit harder to hide decal film on foil compared to paint, so you have two options. You can apply the lettering as a single piece and live with a bit of

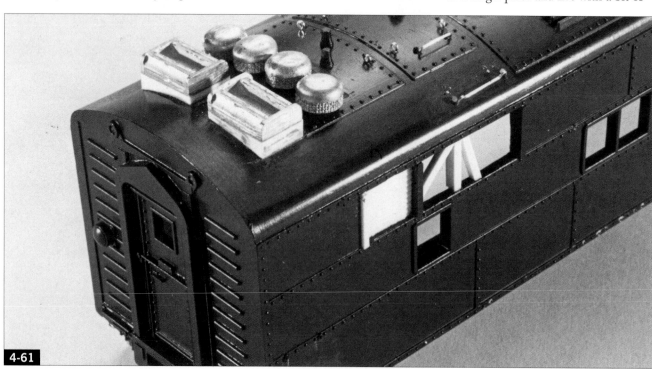

4-61

Add bracing to the openings. The rear square opening uses clapboard siding to simulate louvers.

decal film showing, or you can cut the decal into individual letters and apply them separately. Although this takes more time and effort, you'll eliminate the decal film between letters.

The model's number boards are designed to be lighted from behind, but the numbers are difficult to see in normal lighting. I decided to cover them with ShellScale number board decals, and I renumbered the model as an E9.

Other decal details include the E9 model designation plates and EMD builder's plates from Microscale set 87-527.

E7 modifications

The E7 model, **4-58**, followed most of the same steps as the E9. You could do this with a decorated Proto 2000 model, but I started this model long ago, using an old Model Power shell atop a Proto Power West chassis and painting and decaling the shell before adding the Bare-Metal Foil.

The E7s differed from the E8s and E9s in having screened side openings at the top of the shell instead of stainless steel grilles. Capturing the see-through look of the real things requires a bit of cutting and fitting, but results in a more realistic look.

Remove material from the molded screens by drilling them out, **4-59**. Be careful not to drill into the surrounding frame. Use a hobby knife to finish trimming plastic out of the openings to the edge of the frames, **4-60**.

Some E7s had an additional square air intake behind the rear-most standard opening. To add this, drill a hole behind the rear screen, carve it square using a hobby knife, and frame the opening with styrene strip to match the other openings, **4-61**. Evergreen clapboard siding, glued in place behind this opening, simulates louvers.

Model the bracing visible behind these screens with .060"-square styrene strip and paint them silver. Cut Detail Associates screen material to fit in each opening. Paint these silver, then glue them in place with small drops of CA on the bracing. Secure them by adding drops of CA around the edges of the screens from inside the shell, **4-62**.

4-62

Glue the screen in place over the bracing in the openings.

4-63

The Burlington's late E7s had two tall vents at the rear, with four screened air intakes in front of them.

Passenger diesels were equipped with a variety of steam generators, and some engines had multiple generators. Variations abound in the number and placement of rooftop steam-generator stacks, vents, and air intakes.

The Burlington's late E7s had two square vents at the rear and four screened air intakes in front of them across the roof panel, **4-63**. The vents are metal castings, but they needed deeper bases to match the roof contour. Make these from several pieces of styrene sheet, cut to match the footprint of the vent, and laminated to a total height of .100".

Place a piece of coarse (120-grit) sandpaper face up on a bare area of the roof, and rub the base across it until it matches the contour of the roof. Smooth the bottoms with finer sandpaper, then glue the vents and stacks in place on the rear roof panel.

I weathered both models following the guidelines in chapter 5. Since passenger engines were often kept cleaner than freight locomotives, I kept the weathering fairly light – an overspray of grimy black on the roof to simulate exhaust residue, and some grimy black and earth colors on the pilot, trucks, and lower sides.

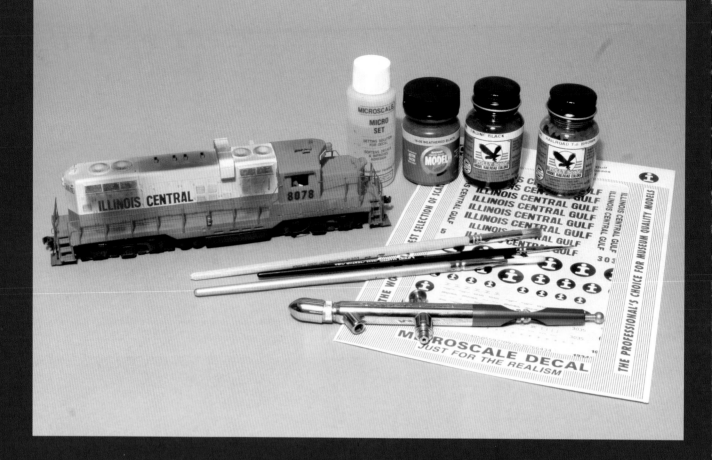

CHAPTER FIVE

Fresh paint, old look

Learning to paint and add decals allows you to finish undecorated models. It can also enhance the realism of your decorated models with new details and weathering.

Most locomotive models today feature sharp, accurate paint and lettering. However, if you look closely at your existing roster of locomotives, you may find opportunities to improve their detail and realism with decals and paint. Furthermore, mastering these skills should give you the confidence to tackle more-specialized units you can't find commercially.

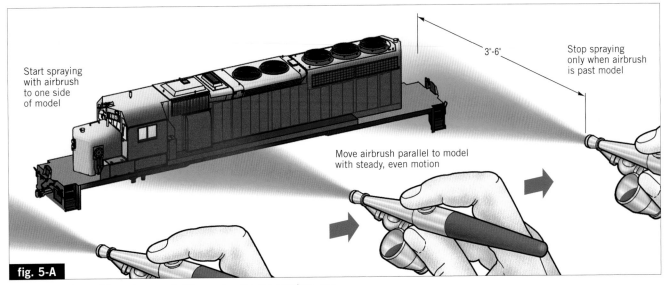

Use even strokes, with each pass slightly overlapping the previous one.

Sometimes you have to paint

When you modify a model extensively (as with the Paducah rebuild in chapter 4), your only option is to paint the entire locomotive. Also, if the paint scheme you need isn't available on a particular model, you'll have to consider a new paint job.

Painting intimidates many modelers, but by taking the process slowly and practicing your technique, you can acquire the necessary skills.

Airbrushing is the subject for a book in itself, and for a more detailed description of the technique, see *Basic Painting and Weathering for Model Railroaders*, published by Kalmbach Publishing Co. For now, let's go through the painting process step-by-step, using the IC diesel as an example.

Preparation

The first step in preparing your model for paint is to think about what parts get which paints. That way, you can paint as many of the parts as possible at the same time in subassemblies. For example, if the cab is a different color than the hood, paint them separately, then put them together. Other times it's easiest to assemble the model first, as with this model.

Surface preparation is extremely important. In handling the model, oils from your fingers, as well as general dust and grime, accumulate on the shell. If contaminants aren't removed, the paint won't stick well to the surface

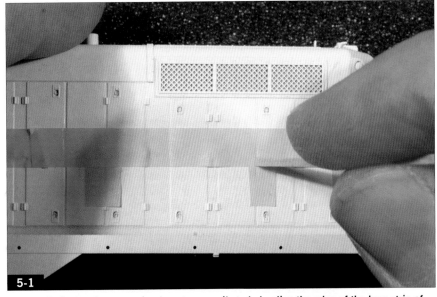

5-1 The small pieces of tape are in place temporarily to help align the edge of the long strip of tape. Use a toothpick to press the tape firmly into crevices and around details.

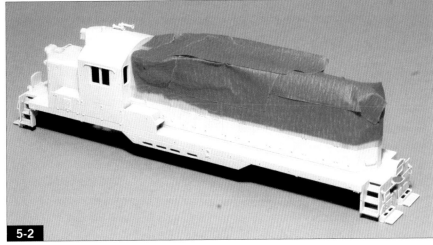

5-2 Cover the remaining masked areas with wide tape. Double-check to make sure the entire masked area is sealed and that the edge is burnished tightly to the model.

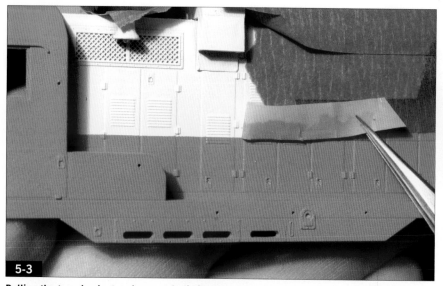

5-3

Pulling the tape back at a sharp angle limits the stress on the underlying paint. The tight tape joint resulted in a sharply defined paint separation line.

5-4

A shallow jar lid works well for holding water for decaling.

5-5

A clear drafting triangle used as a straightedge lets you see your progress while cutting decals.

5-6

Curved scissors are best for cutting circular and oval-shaped heralds.

in some areas, and dust or fingerprints can show through the finish. Use an old toothbrush to scrub the model thoroughly with warm water and liquid dish detergent, then rinse the shell under warm running water until all traces of the soap are gone. Place the model in a dust-free area and allow it to dry completely.

An airbrush is the best way to obtain a smooth, even finish. Apply paint in light coats, making sure the paint is wet when it hits the model, but not so thick that the paint puddles or runs. Start the airbrush off one edge of the shell, then move it steadily across the model, not releasing the air until the spay is past the end, 5-A. Repeat the process, slightly overlapping the strokes.

An advantage of acrylic paints is that you can accelerate drying the paint between coats with a hair dryer. Go over the model thoroughly, and once the paint dries, add the next coat. Vary the airbrush angle to get into all nooks and crannies and hit all sides of all details. Check the model under a bright light to make sure the paint has completely covered the model.

Orange and white found in the IC model – are notoriously poor-covering colors. Also, the shell was light gray, but some detail parts were a mix of brass and dark-color plastic, so I decided to give the model a light primer coat of light gray (ModelFlex

No. 1612 Primer Gray) to provide a uniform color base for the final colors. This step is usually not necessary if you're applying darker colors such as blue, green, maroon, black, or gray.

Use the manufacturers' specified thinning ratios as a starting point. I've had good results mixing Polly Scale colors with about 30 percent Polly S Airbrush Thinner, spraying it at about 18 psi. For ModelFlex paints, I spray straight from the bottle or thinned with about 10 percent distilled water and flowing at about 20 psi.

Once the gray is dry, apply the white. Although the white area only covers the upper part of the long hood, I airbrushed the entire model white to give the orange a uniform base color. The white will also tend to brighten the following orange coat.

Masking

Masking is probably the most important step in any multi-color paint scheme. A poor mask job will result in paint bleeding under the tape, a problem that often can't be fixed.

Check the location of paint division lines following prototype photos or lettering diagrams. Reference points on the model, such as louvers and door hinges, can help guide your masking. The IC engine has a single straight line around the hood, which at first seems easy to mask, but it crosses many doors near hinges and over louvers, which can be a challenge.

I prefer 3M Fineline masking tape. It's narrow, easy to handle, provides a sharp, clean edge, sticks well without the risk of peeling off underlying paint, and it flexes enough to go over details. Small sections of tape serve as reference points along the separation line, **5-1**, to help guide the tape into position.

Use a toothpick with a chisel point to burnish the tape around details such as door edges and seams. Never use metal tools (such as tweezers) for this, as they will scratch the paint. You might have to cut narrower strips to fit tight areas or work around protruding details.

Once the tape is in place, double-check to make sure it's straight. If it's

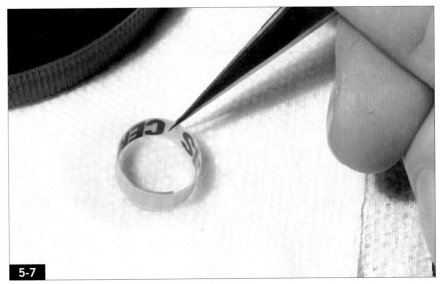
5-7
Remove the decal from the water and place it on a paper towel. Long decals will curl at first.

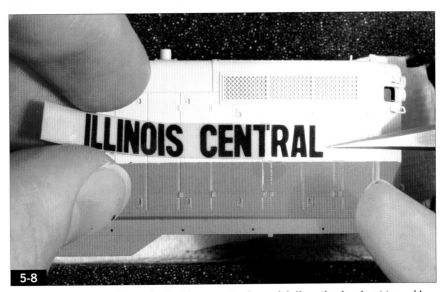
5-8
Carefully slide the decal from the backing paper to the model. Keep the decal wet to avoid tearing it.

5-9
Use a soft brush to nudge the decal into position. Apply decal setting solution around the edges, being careful not to move the decal.

5-10

The decal will wrinkle as the setting solution goes to work, but it will lay flat when the solution evaporates.

5-11

Once the decal is dry, wipe away any stains from decal solution with a damp cotton swab.

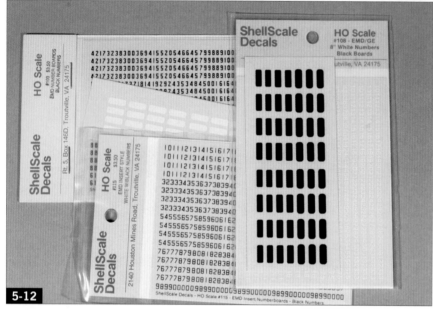

5-12

ShellScale offers a wide range of number board decals for contemporary and early diesels.

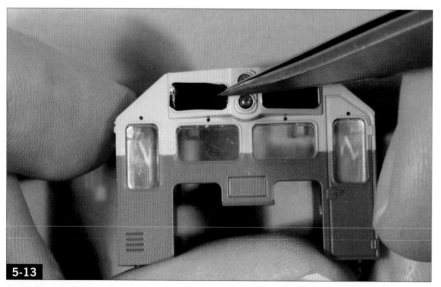

5-13

Apply the number board background first, then let it dry completely before adding the numerals.

not, take a deep breath, peel off the tape and start over. Wavy paint lines stand out on models and are impossible to fix short of repainting.

Fill in the remaining area with wider strips of common masking tape, **5-2**, making sure that the entire masked area is covered. Immediately prior to painting the second color, re-burnish the tape along the entire separation line with a toothpick.

Apply the second paint color in much the same manner as the first, but make sure the first two coats are light, and make sure the airbrush is aimed away from the tape edge to reduce the chance of paint bleeding through. The first light coats will seal the tape edge, and you can then direct the airbrush as needed.

Remove the masking as soon as possible after painting. With acrylics, going over the model a couple of minutes with a hair dryer is sufficient; by the time you've cleaned your airbrush, the paint will be cured. You'll need to wait longer for solvent-based paints or spray cans.

Pulling the tape back against itself at a sharp angle, **5-3**, reduces the stress on the underlying paint. Provided the initial surface was clean, you shouldn't have problems with paint pulling off.

Few paint jobs go on perfectly. You'll probably find a couple of spots where paint bled through a bit or where the airbrush didn't quite reach. Neither situation is usually serious. Simply touch up the areas with a fine-point brush.

5-14

The Microscale decal herald is much more accurate than the factory-applied herald on the Kato model.

Decal basics

Most modern decals have a thin transfer film and when applied properly, they're nearly invisible after they're in place – especially if given a clear overcoat.

The key is to apply decals only to gloss or semi-gloss surfaces. A decal placed over a flat finish will "silver," a condition where tiny air pockets have been trapped under the decal surface. If a model has a flat finish, spray clear gloss finish over the area to be decaled.

Always use distilled water when decaling. Tap water contains minerals and other impurities that will remain on your model when the water evaporates. An old, shallow jar lid works well for holding water, 5-4. Dark lids make it easy to spot white decals that have floated off their backing paper.

Start by cutting the decal from its backing paper with small sharp scissors or a fresh hobby knife. A dull knife will leave a ragged edge that will show after the decal is applied. A clear drafting triangle as a cutting guide, 5-5, makes it easy to see the cut line without hiding the lettering. Fine scissors are best for curved decals such as heralds, 5-6.

Dip the decal in water for about 10 seconds with tweezers, then place the decal on a paper towel, 5-7. Long decals tend to curl – that's OK, just leave them alone.

In the meantime, use a brush to paint a puddle of Microscale Micro Set on the model at the decal location. This weak setting solution will help the decal start to set on the model, but still allows time to work with the decal. The decal will start to release from its

5-15

Scrape away the old herald with the edge of a hobby knife, being careful not to scrape away the body paint.

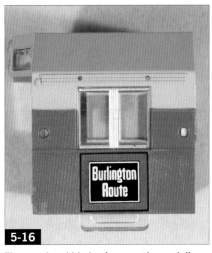

5-16

The new herald helps improve the model's realism.

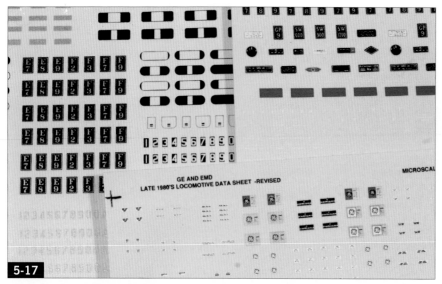

5-17

Microscale decal set no. 87-527 includes number boards, modern builder's plates, class light gaskets, and warning labels.

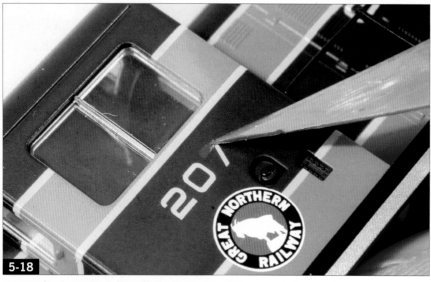

5-18

Use the tip of a hobby knife, laid flat, to scrape off the unwanted numeral.

5-19

Replace the old numeral with an appropriate decal.

backing paper in 30 seconds to a minute. Guide the decal in one hand while sliding it onto the model using tweezers or a toothpick, **5-8**. Get the decal in its proper location, but don't worry about exact placement yet.

A paintbrush works well for fine maneuvers to get the decal into position, **5-9**. Keep the decal wet while doing this. If it begins to stick, add more water or Micro Set until it slides.

Once the decal is in place, leave it alone until most of the water and setting solution have evaporated. You can remove water by touching the decal with a corner of a paper towel, but you risk moving the decal by doing so.

You're now ready to fix the decal to the model with a strong setting solution. I prefer Microscale Micro Set for most decals; some thicker decals (notably from Champ) might require a stronger solution such as Walthers Solvaset or Champ Decal Set. Load a brush with solution and carefully touch it around the edges of the decal. Capillary action will draw the fluid under the decal.

The solution will soften the decal, allowing it to mold itself over details such as hinges, latches, and louvers. Leave the decal alone while it's softening; trying to adjust it will tear the decal, requiring you to start over. Although the decal will wrinkle while the solution works, **5-10**, it will smooth out when it dries.

When the decal is dry, carefully slice any bubbles or air pockets with a hobby knife, and apply more setting solution to that area. Repeat the process until the entire decal is firmly on the surface.

The setting solution might leave some marks on the surface after the decal has dried. Remove these marks by rubbing them lightly with a damp cotton swab, **5-11**.

Seal the decals and blend them with the surface by giving the model a light clear flat or satin overcoat. I used Polly Scale Flat Finish, thinned with about 40 percent Polly S Airbrush Thinner.

Decal details

Decals offer many opportunities to upgrade decorated models. Number boards are among the easiest details to

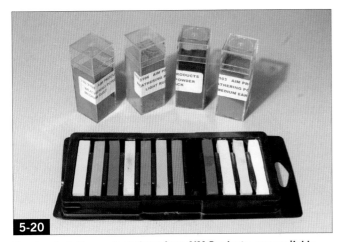

5-20

Powdered chalks, such as those from AIM Products, are available commercially, or you can make your own from artist's pastel chalks.

5-21

Apply chalk with a stiff brush. Touch the bristles to the powder, then dab and brush the chalk on the model.

add to models. You can add them to a model without number boards, upgrade the number boards to a more-accurate style, or renumber a model.

Prototype number boards come in a variety of distinctive styles depending upon builder, railroad, and era. Shell-Scale offers several styles of numbers to match these variations, **5-12**, and Microscale offers many as well.

Start by applying the number board background, which is either a white or black panel, **5-13**. Use setting solution on the panel, then let it dry completely. You can then safely add the numerals without damaging the background panel.

The factory-decorated Burlington GP35 in chapter 2 had generally good paint and lettering, but the cab herald was inaccurate, **5-14**, having incorrect lettering and borders. Start by getting a new decal herald (this one from Microscale set no. 87-15).

Although applying the new decal directly over the old herald is tempting, most decals aren't completely opaque, meaning some of the old herald could show through the decal. Also, in this case, the model's herald was slightly larger than the decal.

Instead, remove the old herald by scraping it with the edge of a hobby knife, **5-15**. By going slowly, it's usually

possible to remove the herald without scraping through the underlying paint. Once that's done, apply the herald like any other decal, **5-16**.

Other models throughout this book show examples of decal details, including model designation plates (on the Burlington E units in chapter 4) and builder's plates, **5-17** (the Burlington E units and GP35, as well as the IC GP10).

Renumbering models

Many models are offered with multiple road numbers; others only have a single number, or perhaps don't reflect the number you want to model. For

5-22

Black and dark gray chalks simulate soot from diesel exhaust.

5-23

Dust and rust chalk colors highlight details on black truck sideframes.

Weathering

Freshly painted locomotives don't look that way for long. Soot from exhaust, road grime kicked up by the wheels, and rust and weathered paint all take their toll.

Some railroads are more picky about keeping their locomotives clean and even repaint them every few years. Other railroads let appearance go, with faded and peeling lettering, grime, and rust obscuring the paint.

Many materials and techniques work well for weathering, including chalks, model paint, paint washes, and artist's crayons. The key is to observe real locomotives and photos and determine the best methods for capturing the look on a model.

Dust, rust, and grime

Two effective ways of capturing the look of overall grime, dust, and soot are applying powdered chalk and spraying thinned mists of grime- or dust-colored paint.

Chalks don't require an airbrush or special equipment. They're easy to apply and work with and quite forgiving. Chalk powders in weathering colors are available from several manufacturers, **5-20**, or you can use artist's pastel chalks (don't use cheap kids' playground chalk) to make your own. Scrape the chalk with a hobby knife and collect the powder in a small container like an old film canister.

example, the Great Northern RS-2 in chapter 2 was numbered 207. However, that number, although accurate, reflected a prototype engine with a steam generator – a detail the model doesn't have, and one that I didn't want to add. I matched the model's details to a prototype photo of No. 201, so I needed to change the model's number to match it.

The method that works best for me is to carefully scrape off the existing number with a hobby knife, **5-18**. More care is needed than when removing the herald, because the area will remain in view.

Keep the blade flat to the surface while using just the tip to scrape the numeral, and work slowly. Practice this technique on an old shell before trying it on a good model. If any body paint gets scratched, touch it up with matching paint.

Apply the new number – in this case, I used a "1" from a Microscale set for GN diesels (No. 87-815), **5-19**. You can simply replace individual numerals if the color and style of the decal and factory-applied lettering match. If they vary, then it's best to remove and reapply all of the numerals in the number.

Other methods for removing numbers are rubbing them with a pencil or ink eraser and using an eraser dipped in decal solution or paint remover. These methods tend to remove paint, requiring more paint touch up.

5-24

Weathering with colors for road dust should be low on locomotive sides.

Weathering colors that are always handy to have on hand include various shades of gray and black for soot and general grime; browns, ochres, and deep reds for rust; and light yellows, tans, and beige for dust. It's easy to mix these colors to get the effect you're looking for.

A common fear of working with chalk is that it's easy to blow away your beautiful weathering effects with a blast of clear coat sprayed over them. The key to avoiding this is to apply chalks to a dead-flat finish, which gives the chalk some "tooth" to grab. If a model has a gloss or satin finish, give it a light coat of clear flat and let it dry before applying chalk. If you don't, the chalk will indeed blow away when you try to seal it.

I prefer a stiff brush for applying chalk, **5-21**. Hog bristle brushes are inexpensive and work well. Touch the bristles into the chalk, then use a combination of dabbing and stroking to apply chalk to the model. Chalk looks great as exhaust soot, **5-22**, and for adding grime and rust colors to couplers, pilots, and truck sideframes, **5-23**.

You can also use chalk to add dust patterns to locomotive ends and sides. For example, cab unit diesels tend to kick up grime directly above the lead truck in a pattern that feathers out along the sides. This is easy to duplicate with chalk, **5-24**.

Be careful not to touch the model once you've applied chalk. Seal chalk weathering with a clear flat or semi-gloss overcoat. I prefer Polly Scale clear flat or clear satin applied with an airbrush, but spray cans also work. I've had good luck with Model Master's clear satin spray.

If you have an airbrush, many of these dust, rust, and grime effects can be obtained by spraying thinned mixes (about one part paint and nine parts thinner) of weathering colors such as black, grimy black, rail brown, and railroad tie brown. Apply these mixes in very light coats, building up the effect gradually and using multiple colors for different effects, **5-25**.

Two other areas to hit with paint are exhaust stacks and wheels. Use a fine brush to paint the insides of

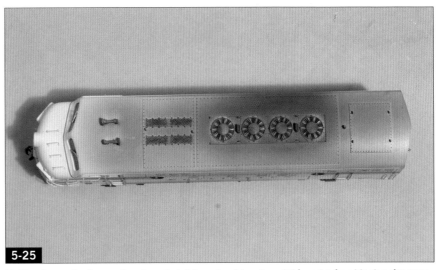

5-25

Light-color roofs show exhaust-soot staining. An airbrush and thinned grimy black paint gave this roof a fairly uniform coat of grime.

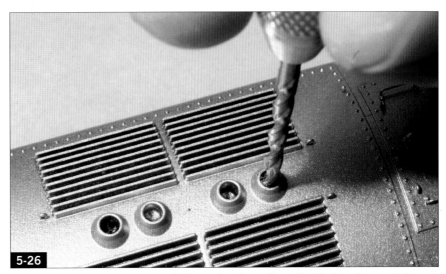

5-26

Drilling out exhaust stacks, then painting the interior surfaces flat black, enhances their appearance.

5-27

Paint wheel faces a flat, dark rust color such as rail brown or railroad tie brown, then paint the shiny truck frames flat black.

5-28

Apply a thinned paint wash to grills with a brush.

5-29

When it dries, the wash gives grills and screened areas the appearance of depth.

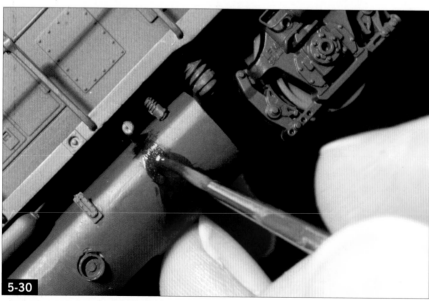

5-30

Apply oily black paint around the fuel fillers and fuel tanks on some models.

exhaust stacks flat black. Although it doesn't exactly qualify as weathering, drilling out exhaust stacks when possible enhances their appearance, **5-26**.

Before weathering trucks, remove the sideframes and paint the wheels a rust color, **5-27**. Many models have inner truck frames of shiny metal – painting these flat black will help hide them from view.

Washes and grills

Washes of thinned paint are another great way of creating special effects. Thin paint the same way as for weathering sprays – about nine parts thinner to one part paint. I prefer Polly Scale acrylic paints, thinned with Polly S Airbrush Thinner. This alcohol-based thinner is great for washes, as it has a lower surface tension than water, which tends to bead.

Washes are especially effective for highlighting grills, **5-28**, as the washes tend to stay in recessed areas, giving

5-31

This **GN** RS-2 received a number of weathering treatments, including grimy black washes in the side louvers, black and grimy black weathering sprays on the roof, sides, trucks, and pilots, rust and dust chalks on the truck sideframes, light washes over the horizontal white stripe on the frame, and a light fuel stain below the filler on the cab side.

them a look of depth, **5-29**. The IC model on page 68 has also had washes (along with chalk weathering) applied below its side grills to simulate oily residue that rain has washed down the side of the locomotive.

Artist's oil paints have become popular for weathering in recent years. They can be applied as washes by dipping a brush in turpentine or mineral spirits, touching the brush to the paint, and applying it to the model. Burnt umber, burnt sienna, raw umber, and Mars black all work well for weathering.

An advantage of oil paint washes is that they're easier to control than acrylic washes as the paint will remain workable for quite awhile. If you don't like an effect, you can remove it by going over the area with clear mineral spirits.

You can also apply full-strength paint for various effects. One example is brushing oily black paint (such as Polly Scale No. 414326) around fuel fillers, **5-30**, to simulate fuel spills. Mix it up by applying it subtly on some models and heavily on others. It's most effective after other weathering.

Don't become too dependent on a single weathering material or technique. Combining multiple methods usually results in the most-realistic models, **5-31**.

Handrails

Starting in the 1960s, railroads began painting the vertical corner step handrails a contrasting color. Some manufacturers offer models with this feature; others don't, but you can easily upgrade them. Don't automatically reach for the white paint: Some railroads used yellow or other colors, and other railroads painted all handrails/stanchions a color that contrasted with the body. Also double-check the overall handrail color, as manufacturers don't always get it correct.

Getting paint to stick to engineering-plastic handrails is always a challenge. One of the best paints for the purpose is Pactra Racing Finish lacquer. It's a flexible, chip-resistant paint designed for painting clear Lexan R/C car bodies, and it's available in several colors. Use a brush to paint the handrails following prototype photos or diagrams. Getting paint all the way around the handrail, so that paint encapsulates the handrail, will help it keep a firm grip on the part.

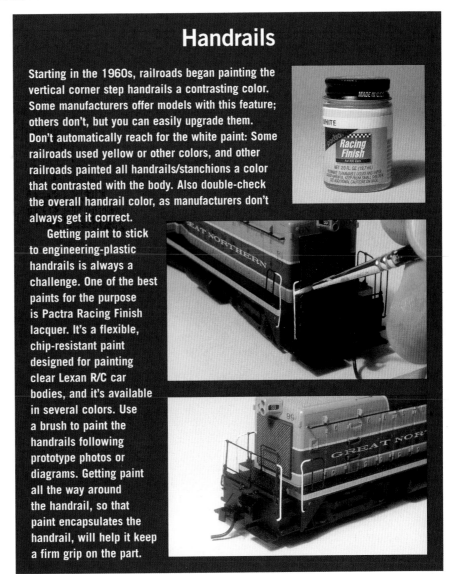

CHAPTER SIX

Well-connected couplers

Horn-hook couplers have given way to realistic, smooth-operating designs such as the Kadee Magne-Matic.

Locomotive couplers have to be tough. They must be strong enough to withstand the constant buffeting from multiple powered locomotives operating in a consist and strong enough to pull the weight of the entire train. Since locomotives tend to receive more attention than rolling stock, it's important that couplers look realistic as well.

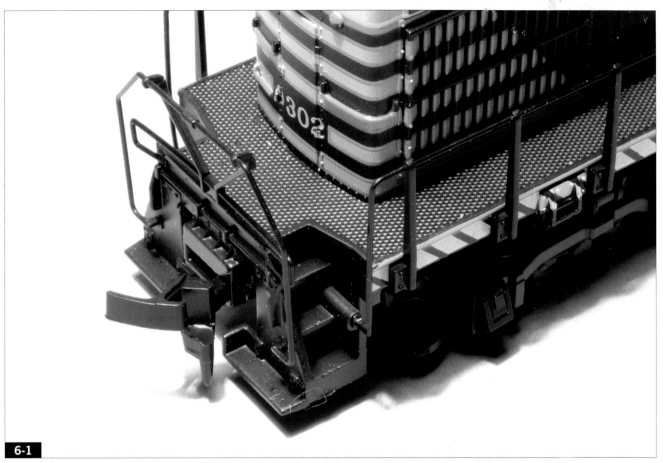

6-1

The horn-hook coupler was standard equipment on most locomotives through the 1990s. The design suffered both operationally and visually.

De-horning your couplers

Into the 1990s, the horn-hook coupler, 6-1, was standard equipment on HO locomotives and freight cars. The design was free to any manufacturer and inexpensive to produce. Unfortunately horn-hook couplers are difficult to uncouple and tend to skew to the side during pushing. Even worse is that they bear little resemblance to real couplers and are especially ugly on locomotives, where they're are so exposed.

6-2

Knuckle couplers include, clockwise from top left, No. 58 scale coupler; No. 5 coupler in box with mounting tabs trimmed; No. 78 scale coupler with scale draft-gear box; No. 33 short-shank coupler; and No. 8 coupler.

6-3

Coupler shanks come in short and extended length, as these No. 33 (foreground) and No. 37 couplers show.

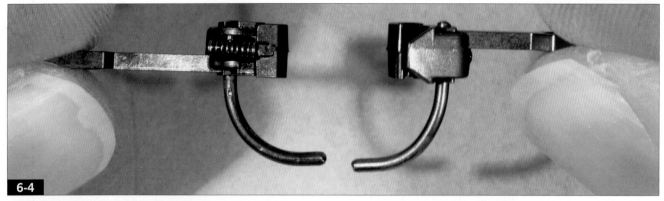

6-4

You can adjust coupler height by changing to couplers with shanks under-set or over-set relative to the knuckle, such as the Kadee No. 27 and No. 22.

6-5

Avoid couplers that with plastic leaf knuckle springs.

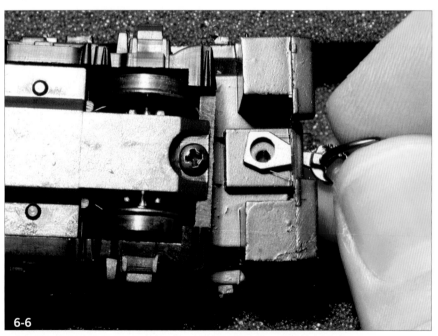

6-6

The Kadee No. 158 coupler with side-mounted centering springs was a good choice for this Atlas switcher. The mounting pad is part of the cast-metal chassis; a plastic cover snaps over the pad.

For these reasons, most serious modelers long ago converted their rolling stock to Kadee automatic knuckle couplers (see photo, opposite page). These operate smoothly, couple easily, and maintain alignment when pushing cars. Uncoupling can be accomplished easily using mechanical means (an uncoupling pick or stick inserted between the knuckles) or magnetically, using between-rails or under-track magnets to activate the uncoupling pins that hang below the knuckles.

In the mid-1990s, as many of Kadee's original patents expired, other manufacturers introduced similar knuckle couplers that mated with Kadee couplers. These include the McHenry, Accurail Accumate, and Bachmann E-Z Mate.

The latest coupler revolution has been size, as Kadee and others now offer scale-size versions of their standard couplers.

Kadee offers the widest variety, with couplers in dozens of variations to fit different mounting situations, 6-2. The key differences among the various styles are the shank length (generally short, medium, or long), 6-3, the over-set or under-set placement of the knuckle on the shank, 6-4, and the shape and depth of the coupler box. I highly recommend Kadee's No. 13 coupler sampler set, which includes examples of most of the couplers the company makes. Having this set makes it easy to test various coupler/coupler box combinations.

Although I used Kadee couplers in the following installations, you can easily substitute those from other mak-

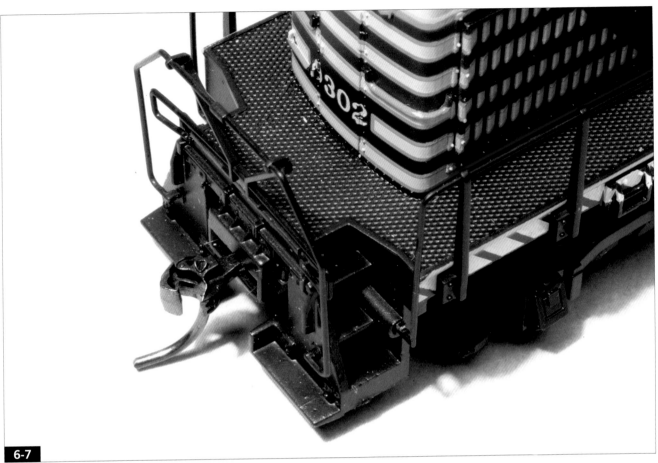

6-7

The new knuckle coupler looks and works much better than the original horn-hook.

ers. The one style to avoid or replace are couplers that use plastic leaf springs to hold the knuckle in place, **6-5**. They tend to lose their spring action, especially if the coupler is accidentally stuck in an open position for an extended time (such as on a siding on a grade). Stick with couplers that have metal coil knuckle springs or those with a split-shank design (Accurail).

Choosing a coupler

Coupler installation varies widely among manufacturers and types of models. Converting most contemporary locomotives – those already

6-8

This Kato GP35 received a Kadee No. 5 coupler in its own box.

6-9

The original Kato friction pin holds the coupler box in place.

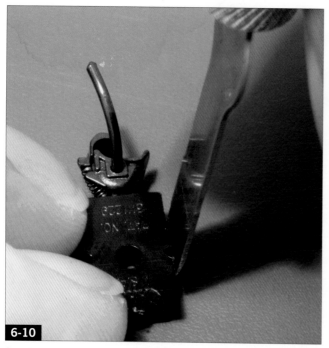

6-10

Cut off the side mounting tabs if the center hole is used for mounting the coupler box.

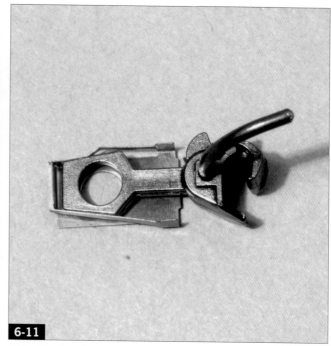

6-11

Kadee No. 5 series couplers' bronze centering spring is designed to rest inside a coupler box.

equipped with knuckle couplers – to Kadee couplers is generally easy, as the body- or frame-mounted coupler box is already designed for a knuckle coupler. For some older locomotives, especially those that came with horn-hook couplers, the process is more difficult.

With any conversion, keep in mind that usually there isn't a single correct solution, as more than one coupler or mounting method will work. The important thing is that when installed, the coupler works smoothly, is at the proper height, and is the proper length.

Many times it's possible to use the locomotive's existing coupler box. Provided that the coupler works well and moves freely, this is usually the best choice. To replace the horn-hook coupler on the Atlas switcher in **6-1**, I removed the coupler box cover, **6-6**, and added a Kadee No. 158, a scale-size coupler with built-in "whisker" springs on the sides. Because the model's coupler box cover snapped in place over a metal mounting pad on the frame (instead of being a separate box),

6-12

The coupler boxes extend from the bodies of these Proto 1000 F units, and the coupler shanks are too long, resulting in an unrealistically wide gap between locomotives.

6-13

These Stewart F units are equipped with Kadee's No. 450 conversion kit and couplers, which tightened the gap to prototypical spacing.

6-14

The shallow No. 33 box works well in locomotive pilots, as on this Proto 1000 F unit.

the one-piece coupler/spring was easier to work with than trying to add the usual coupler with bronze spring, **6-7**.

The Kato GP35 featured in chapter 2 received a Kadee No. 5 coupler in its own box, **6-8**, which fit neatly in the slot in its pilot. Kato models use a heavy friction pin to hold coupler boxes in place, **6-9**. The center mount-ing hole is almost always used for installing this box, so the side mount-ing ears can usually be cut off, **6-10**.

Kadee's No. 5 box will work with any of the Kadee common-shank couplers that use the bronze centering spring, **6-11**, so if this mounting system will work, you can substitute any of Kadee's common couplers with long or short shanks or under-set or over-set shanks.

The Proto 1000 F unit from chapter 2 had a leaf-spring coupler, with a shank that extended too far from the locomotive. The result is too much gap between locomotives (or the locomotive and adjoining car), **6-12**. Tightening the spac-

6-15

Drill the hole with a No. 50 bit to prepare it for a 2-56 mounting screw.

6-16

Use a 2-56 tap to cut threads in the hole for the mounting screw.

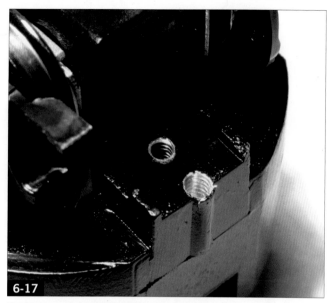

6-17

You can see the threads inside the newly tapped mounting hole.

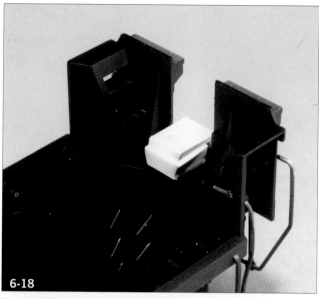

6-18

You can build up layers of sheet styrene to make a coupler mounting pad behind a locomotive pilot. Vary the styrene thickness as needed so the coupler is mounted at the proper height, then drill and tap a mounting hole.

6-19

A Kadee No. 8 coupler worked well on this Athearn model. Make sure the coupler box clears the truck swing.

6-20

For better appearance, you may want to remove the uncoupling pin with heavy side cutters, then file down the area if needed.

6-21

Regardless of the installation, the coupler must be at the correct height for smooth operation. Check each installation with a Kadee gauge, making sure the tops of the couplers match.

ing results in more-realistic spacing between cars or engines and cars, 6-13.

The Kadee No. 5 box wouldn't work on the Proto 1000 model, as the rear of the box would interfere with truck motion. Instead I chose a No. 33 coupler with short shank. The 30-series of couplers has a shank spring that wraps around the center post, with ends that touch the coupler shank on each side, 6-14. This allows for a very shallow coupler box, making it an ideal choice for tight spaces.

The original coupler on this model used the inbound mounting hole, but

Manufacturers

A-Line
P.O. Box 2701
Carlsbad, CA 92018-2701
www.ppw-aline.com

American Model Builders
1420 Hanley Industrial Ct.
St. Louis, MO 63144
www.laserkit.com

Athearn (Div. of Horizon Hobby)
1550 Glenn Curtiss St.
Carson, CA 90746
www.athearn.com

Atlas Model Railroad Co.
378 Florence Ave.
Hillside, NJ 07205
www.atlasrr.com

Cal-Scale (Div. of Bowser Mfg.)
P.O. Box 322
Montoursville, PA 17754
www.bowser-trains.com

Cannon & Co.
310 Willow Heights
Aptos, CA 95003-9798

Champion Decal Co.
P.O. Box 1178
Minot, ND 58702
www.minot.com/~champ/

Custom Finishing
379 Tully Rd.
Orange, MD 01364
(see Wm. K. Walthers)

Detail Associates
(see Wm. K. Walthers)

Details West
www.detailswest.com

Floquil (see Testor Corp.)

Kadee
673 Avenue C
White City, OR 97503-1078
www.kadee.com

Kato USA
100 Remington Rd.
Schaumburg, IL 60173
www.katousa.com

Micro-Mark
340 Snyder Ave.
Berkeley Heights, NJ 07922
www.micromark.com

Microscale
18435 Bandilier Cir.
Fountain Valley, CA 92708
www.microscale.com

Miniatronics
561-K Acorn St.
Deer Park, NY 11729
www.miniatronics.com

MV Products
P.O. Box 6622
Orange, CA 92863

Polly Scale (see Testor Corp.)

Proto 2000 (see Wm. K. Walthers)

Precision Scale Co.
3961 Hwy. 93 N., Box 278
Stevensville, MT 59870

ShellScale Decals
516 Houston Mines Rd.
Troutville, VA 24175
www.shellscale.com

Smokey Valley Railroad Products
P.O. box 339
Plantersville, MS 38862
www.smokeyvalley.com

Sunrise Enterprises
P.O. Box 172
Doyle, CA 96109
www.sunrisenterprises.com

Testor Corp.
440 Blackhawk Park Ave.
Rockford, IL 61104
www.testors.com

Wm. K. Walthers
P.O. Box 3039
Milwaukee, WI 53201-3039
www.walthers.com

the new box required using the outward hole on the pilot end. This hole, however, wasn't tapped for a mounting screw. To use it, I enlarged the hole slightly, **6-15**, with a No. 50 bit. I then tapped the hole for a 2-56 screw, **6-16**.

To cut threads with a tap, place the tap in the hole and begin turning it clockwise until you feel resistance. Back it out a turn or two, then turn it into the hole again. Keep repeating the process until the threads are cut past the depth of your mounting screw, **6-17**.

You can use the above technique for drilling and tapping a mounting hole any time you have a plastic or metal mounting pad and need to create or relocate a mounting hole.

Older Athearn models had coupler mounting pads that extended from the cast metal frame. A common conversion for these was to cut the mounting pad from the frame with a hacksaw, then build up a new mounting pad behind the pilot on the shell using styrene, **6-18**. Tight-clearance coupler boxes, such as the Nos. 8 and 33, are appropriate for these installations, **6-19**.

For the sake of appearance, many modelers cut the uncoupling pins from their locomotive couplers (and some even from freight-car couplers), **6-20**. The couplers will still connect just fine, although a manual uncoupling tool will be needed.

Use a Kadee coupler gauge to check each coupler before adding a model to your layout, **6-21**. Couplers (especially scale-size versions) must be at the proper height, or they can fail unexpectedly.

You can adjust coupler height by using shims under mounting boxes or by using couplers with under-set or over-set shanks.

Add realism to your layout!

Detailing Freight Cars
Improve the appearance and performance of your freight cars! Jeff Wilson shows modelers how to improve ready-to-run and kit HO and N freight cars with upgraded details, wheels, couplers, and loads. Perfect for intermediate model railroaders looking to improve their equipment. 8¼ x 10¾; 88 pgs.; 100 color and 50 b&w photos; softcover.
12420 • $18.95

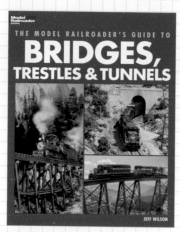

The Model Railroader's Guide to Bridges, Trestles & Tunnels
Each chapter shows prototype examples and ways to model, paint, weather, and install them on a layout. Includes details for numerous types of bridges. Perfect for intermediate and advanced hobbyists. By Jeff Wilson. 8¼ x 10¾; 88 pgs.; 75 color & 100 b&w photos; 15 illus.; softcover.
12452 • $19.95

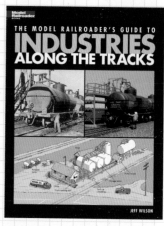

The Model Railroader's Guide to Industries Along the Tracks
Get a look at mining, refining, agricultural operations, and more. Learn techniques for modeling them realistically. By Jeff Wilson. 8¼ x 10¾; 88 pgs.; 50 color and 100 b&w photos; softcover.
12256 • $19.95

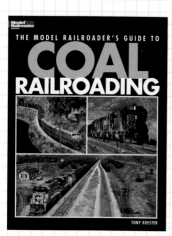

The Model Railroader's Guide to Coal Railroading
A reference for modeling a coal-hauling prototype-based or freelance railroad. Information on modeling coal trains, company towns, and coal customers. By Tony Koester. 8¼ x 10¾; 96 pgs.; 153 color and 66 b&w photos; softcover.
12453 • $19.95

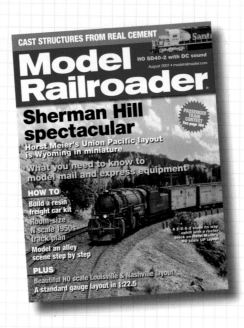

Every issue includes intriguing articles that take you on a tour of the world's finest layouts and introduce you to the hobby's experts. You'll also discover a wealth of prototype data, detailing how-to instructions, product reviews, tips, techniques, and so much more! 12 issues/year.

www. ModelRailroaderBooks.com

Available at hobby shops. To find a store near you visit www.HobbyRetailer.com